10/05 4x

PETIT

soccer

A History of the World's Most Popular Game

MARK STEWART

FRANKLIN WATTS
A Division of Grolier Publishing
New York • London • Hong Kong • Sydney
Danbury, Connecticut

Cover design by Dave Klaboe   Series design by Molly Heron

Photographs ©: Allsport USA: 33 (Al Bello), 81 (Shaun Botterill), 5, 95, 107 (Simon Bruty), cover, inset, 85 left, 89 (David Cannon), 106 (Shaun Dotterill), 103 (Stephen Dunn), 92, 115 (Steve Powell), 66 (Pressens Bild), 96, 116 (Ben Radford), cover inset (Richiardi), 14 (Todd Rosenberg), 85 right (Rick Stewart), cover inset, cover top, 101 (Billy Stickland), cover inset, 39, 43, 61, 62, 74; AP/Wide World Photos: 68, 113; Archive Photos/Popperfoto: 11, 16, 25, 30, 109 bottom, 110; Hulton Getty Images/Tony Stone Images: 7, 10, 12, 17, 18, 45, 55, 112; National Soccer Hall of Fame: 22, 29, 38, 42, 49, 51; Reuters/Corbis-Bettmann: cover insets; SportsChrome East/West: 108 (Brian Drake), 86, 97, 104; UPI/Corbis-Bettmann: 36, 46, 48, 58, 60, 77, 79, 105, 114; archival material courtesy of Team Stewart, Inc.: 24 (National Soccer Hall of Fame), 26, 32 (Blackie & Son, Ltd.), 34 (Gallaher, Ltd.), 52 (Wilson Sporting Goods Co.), 53 (W.D. & H.O. Wills), 54 (left, Barrat & Co., Ltd., left; The Hotspur, right), 59 (Editions Recontre, S.A.), 63 (Editions Recontre, S.A.), 65 (Topical Times), 72 (Edito-Service, S.A.), 73 (A&B Co., Ltd.), 84 (Editions Recontre, S.A.), 93 (Pacific Trading Cards, left and right), 98 (Manchester Union FC), 99 (The Upper Deck Company).

Visit Franklin Watts on the Internet at:
http://publishing.grolier.com

Library of Congress Cataloging-in-Publication Data

Stewart, Mark.
    Soccer: A history of the world's most popular game / Mark Stewart.
    p. cm. — (The Watts history of sports)
    Includes bibliographical references and index.
    Summary: A comprehensive history of soccer, focusing on its evolution,
    momentous events, and key personalities.
    ISBN 0-531-11456-2
    1. Soccer—History—Juvenile literature. [1. Soccer—History.] I. Title. II. Series.
    GV943.25.S84 1998
    796.334—dc21
                                 97-17201
                                    CIP
                                    AC

CONTENTS

THE HISTORY OF SOCCER

In the Beginning

The question of who invented soccer, or where it might first have been played, is difficult to answer. Because the three primary skills involved in the earliest form of the game—running, kicking, and throwing—are among humankind's fundamental physical skills, it is quite likely that some form of soccer has existed in almost every culture at some time in the past. The earliest forerunners of the game were probably rituals in which a ball, representing the sun, was kicked across a newly planted field to ensure a good harvest. The ball itself might have been an animal skin stitched around grass or some other stuffing, or perhaps the actual head of an animal.

The historical record shows that the Chinese played a game called *tsu-shu* during the Han dynasty more than 2,000 years ago. "*Tsu*" means kicking with the foot, and "*shu*" means stuffed leather ball. The game appears in military textbooks, which suggests it was less a game than a training exercise, perhaps to improve the footwork of the emperor's soldiers. Around 1,400 years ago, the Japanese played a similar game, which they called *kemari*. The ancient Greeks enjoyed *episkiros*, which involved kicking and throwing a ball in an area marked by boundary lines. The Romans borrowed this game,

A modern soccer player in Zambia uses a makeshift mud-and-straw ball. Some form of soccer has probably existed in almost every culture at some time.

added a few violent touches of their own, and renamed it *harpastum*. It no doubt spread to other parts of the globe as the Roman empire engulfed most of the western world some 20 centuries ago.

One of the places *harpastum* seems to have been played was Briton, or present-day England, where the Romans ruled for nearly four centuries. The inhabitants of the island were a rough and unruly bunch, and they likely were intrigued by this rough and unruly game. The rules of the day were simple: Players were divided into two teams; a ball was thrown between them; and the team that advanced the ball past the opposite end line was declared the winner. To accomplish this task, contestants were allowed to kick, punch, shove, bite. It was basically an anything-goes affair. Legend has it that in the year 276, residents of the village of Derby took on the Roman legionnaires and beat them at their own game.

When the Romans left England in the year 409, the Britons continued to play this primitive form of soccer for hundreds of years. In rural areas, the men from neighboring villages would square off, with boundaries often stretching a mile or more in every direction. The number of players ranged from a few dozen to a hundred or more, and they laid waste to large areas in their attempt to move the ball toward the opponent's goal line. Initially, the games were held once a year, on Shrove Tuesday, which was the last day to have fun before Lent.

Played out in the fields, this game of "football" might result in a few broken bones, an unfortunate death or two, and

MEANWHILE . . .

Although they did not lead directly to soccer, football-like games were also being played in many other cultures outside the British Isles. The Mayan game of *pokyah* dates back to the seventh century. Played in a specially constructed ball court, it forbid players to touch the ball with their hands, although they were allowed to use their feet, legs, hips, and elbows. A form of this ancient game is still played in many Central American countries. In the 12th century, a game similar to soccer called *le soule* was popular in France. Fourteenth-century Italian explorers reported seeing a game similar to soccer being played during their travels in the Orient, and a rugby-like sport called *giuoco del calcio Fiorentino* was played by Italian aristocrats for nearly four centuries beginning in the 1400s. In 1609—four years after the game was finally legalized in England—a soccer match was played at the Jamestown settlement in Virginia, and 25 years later settler William Wood described a kicking game played by the natives, noting their "swift footmanship" and "strange manipulation of the ball." And far to the north, in what are now Canada and Alaska, the Inuit were playing a form of soccer on ice, which they called *aqsaqtuk*.

A boisterous game of football roars through the streets of an 18th-century English village.

some minor property damage. In the streets of a town or city, however, it presented quite another problem. Indeed, by the 12th century, residents of England's growing villages lived in mortal fear of these contests.

Typically, they began in the central marketplace, with the goals being stationed at opposite ends of town. Two teams would kick or carry a ball through the narrow streets in a scene that resembled a wild mob. There was nothing like a referee present; the concept of an official to keep matters from getting out of hand seemed to defeat the very purpose of the game. Indeed, so frightening was this mob that everyone would barricade themselves in their homes when the players came barreling down the street. Naturally, the worse the conditions, the more people wanted to play. A single game could turn a muddy back street into an impassable quagmire. And

when it snowed, young men took to the streets for one of the wildest winter sports in human history.

The damage done to the pushcarts, kiosks, and shops in these towns was considerable, and in 1314 merchants petitioned King Edward II to do something about this popular game before it put them out of business. On April 13, the king issued a proclamation that banned "hustling over large balls," but the new law had no impact. Twenty-five years later, his son, Edward III, actually ordered his sheriffs to arrest soccer players under the pretense of national security. He believed that his people's passion for this crazy sport was replacing such skills as archery and javelin-throwing. Edward had his eye on conquering France, and he knew that a rowdy band of football players would do him little good on the battlefield.

Royal proclamations had little effect.

ON FOOT, NOT WITH THE FOOT

The term football was in common use in England by the 1400s. Because most respectable sports were played on horseback, the word football actually referred to the fact that this was a game played on foot. Players used a ball that was simple and tough; an inflated pig's bladder was the preferred object.

Many kings and queens tried to ban football, but there was nothing they could do to control what was rapidly becoming England's national pastime. It got so bad that even priests were playing! In 1491, while Christopher Columbus was busy convincing King Ferdinand and Queen Isabella of Spain that they should finance his voyage, their English counterpart, James III, had become convinced that certain athletic activities constituted a threat to the future of his kingdom. Henceforth, he proclaimed, it would be illegal to play "futeball, golfe, or other sik unprofitable sports."

When Oliver Cromwell and the Puritans gained power in England during the mid-1600s, they too tried to outlaw football, even though Cromwell himself had been known to join in the fun while in college. They bemoaned its senseless violence and especially despised the fact that it was regularly played on Sundays. Still, the people played. In fact, writings of the day began to refer to "football" in a bit more detail. The game itself still resembled present-day rugby: Players bunched together; there was a lot of pushing and shoving; and in many regions forward passing was against the rules. But the game was beginning to resemble soccer in other ways, as rules against tripping, charging, and grabbing below the waist began to gain wide acceptance. The ball, too, started to look like its modern descendant: it was an inflated animal bladder encased in leather. The goal usually consisted of two tall sticks set several feet apart, and the distance between goals was remarkably similar to what it is today. The game was still hard and violent, especially when play got close to one of the goals, where it resembled a shin-kicking contest. Because games often ended after a single goal was scored, agility and finesse were not regarded as important qualities. Strong legs, a thick skull, and a general disregard for personal safety were what it took to be a star. Indeed, part of the attraction of these games was the chance to overpower and injure opponents, as well as earning a few scars and bruises yourself. The quick, wiry scorers of modern soccer—Matthews, Pelé, Platini—would not have had much impact in the formative years of soccer. In fact, they might not have been allowed to play at all.

By the 18th century, England was undergoing a remarkable Industrial Revolution. Many people left the country's rural areas and headed for the cities, where work was steady and pay was better. With football all but banned from city streets and the typical work week running from Monday through Saturday, there was little time or opportunity to play. But the sport did not die. Instead, it was taken up by the growing middle and upper classes, who put a slightly more civilized face on this brutal pastime.

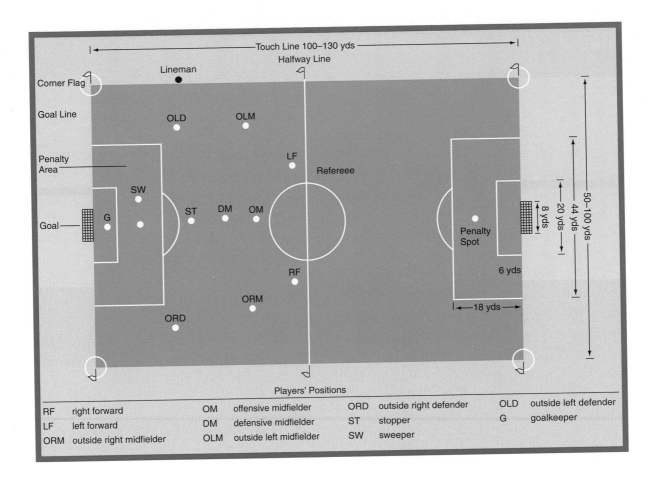

Touch Line 100–130 yds

Halfway Line

Lineman

Corner Flag

Goal Line

OLD OLM

Penalty Area

LF

Refereee

SW

ST DM OM

Goal — G

Penalty Spot

50–100 yds
44 yds
20 yds
8 yds

RF

6 yds

ORM

ORD

18 yds

Players' Positions

RF	right forward	OM	offensive midfielder	ORD	outside right defender	OLD	outside left defender
LF	left forward	DM	defensive midfielder	ST	stopper	G	goalkeeper
ORM	outside right midfielder	OLM	outside left midfielder	SW	sweeper		

The Split

As the 19th century began, football increased in popularity, partly due to the blessing of the church. "Muscular Christianity" was a popular movement in England at the time, and many a Sunday school teacher led his pupils both in prayer and on the playing field.

The game also began to evolve in two different directions during this period. Two of the many effects of the Industrial Revolution were a significant increase in the number of schools in England and the rise of men's clubs, especially in the major cities. Clubs usually were formed by alumni of the same school or by colleagues of the same profession. There were clubs whose memberships consisted of attorneys, accountants, civil servants, or former soldiers. Schools and clubs thrive on organization, and organization depends greatly upon rules. So it was only natural that students and club members would set down the rules of their favorite game, football, and that in doing so each group would create rules best suited to its vision of what this sport should be.

For some, physical contact was an attractive antidote for the monotony of an increasingly civilized world. Their game of football took on the characteristics of modern rugby, with a premium placed on the struggle for physical possession of the ball. Theirs was an exciting, exhilarating contest of pushing, shoving, blocking, and tackling. For others, it seemed only natural that the cooperation, skill, and fair play that they strived for in work characterize the way they played. The major proponents of the latter playing style were students and graduates of some of England's finest schools, including Eton, Harrow, Winchester, and Cambridge. Their game was relatively clean. There were rules against touching the ball with the hands; colliding with and tripping opponents was also forbidden. It was this game that soon evolved into soccer, although during this time, most people were actually playing a game that fell somewhere in between these two extremes.

The evolution of these two versions of the same game into modern soccer and rugby was aided by the rapid transformation England was undergoing. Great Britain had become the world's leading industrial nation, manufacturing goods for Europe, the Americas, and the Far East. To get these goods from factories to ships, a sophisticated network of roads, rails, and canals was developed. Naturally, getting people from one place to another became a lot eas-

ier, too, so the idea of one town challenging another to a football match no longer presented the logistical nightmare it once had. The same went for schools and universities, which had the financial means to travel on a more or less regular basis.

Here were the roots of a "season" or "schedule," but with one obstacle: No one was playing exactly the same game. In fact, even the size and shape of the ball varied from school to school. How could you have a single match, let alone a league or confederation, if you could not decide on the most fundamental rules of play? This interesting tangle of events served to accelerate the division between rugby and soccer, and by the mid-19th century most everyone was playing one game, the other, or both.

The Simplest Game

In 1848, representatives from England's major schools got together and agreed upon a

This mid-19th century illustration shows English school boys playing an informal game of soccer.

basic set of soccer regulations. It took just under eight hours to produce what would come to be known as the Cambridge Rules, and these rules slowly but surely became universally regarded as the definitive rules of soccer. In 1862, J. C. Thring, the Assistant Master at Uppingham, issued the rules for what he called "The Simplest Game." This document is the oldest surviving rule book for soccer. A year later, the major soccer-playing clubs in and around London met at the Freemasons' Tavern to form the first Football Association, "with the object of establishing a definite code of rules for the regulation of the game." The top schools were invited to join the association, and most did. The creation of the Football Association also marked the final and decisive split between soccer and rugby players.

For the next 17 years, soccer flourished all over England and the game began to take a form that would be familiar to fans today. During the 1860s and 1870s, soccer's image made great gains. No longer viewed by the public as thinly veiled mass brutality, the game was starting to gain on cricket and other outdoor sports as a civilized pastime suitable for young men of all classes. It also became a popular spectator sport, especially after 1872, when the Football Association Challenge Cup (or FA Cup, as it is now called) was introduced. It was a single-elimination tournament open to member clubs in the Association, and it served as soccer's first championship.

That same year a team of England's best players met a team of Scotland's best players in history's first international match. The Scots embraced the game with great enthusiasm and played it their own way. Much emphasis was placed on passing, whereas the English focused on individual dribbling skills. The match ended in a scoreless tie, but it provided a glimpse of things to come in a couple of ways. First, it established a method for selecting "national teams" that survives to this day. Second, Scotland played far better than expected. Scottish clubs adhered to the Football Association's 10 basic rules and were considered members in good standing. Their refusal to use the throw-in and their rather liberal interpretation of the offside rule were viewed as minor sticking points. They were known as hard, tough players who could dig deep and come up with a little extra when a match was on the line.

The penalty kick—a one-on-one shot

This hand-colored engraving depicts an 1875 soccer match between England and Scotland.

WORD ASSOCIATION

The term soccer first appeared in the 1870s after the Football Association was founded. Then, as now, some English boys used a form of slang that dropped the end off a word and replaced it with "er." Rugby football thus became "rugger," and Association football became "soccer," borrowing the s-o-c from Association. From that time on, the words soccer and football were used interchangeably, just as basketball and hoops are today. The use of the word soccer in the United States became popular as American football grew in importance. For many years, U.S. fans referred to soccer as soccer-football. In fact, it was not until 1974 that the United States Soccer Football Association rechristened itself the U.S. Soccer Federation.

The 1895 English national team posed for this team photo. Several of the players played both Association football and rugby.

from 12 yards out—was established in 1891 to address violations in the immediate vicinity of the goal. With the penalty kick came the delineation of the penalty area. By 1902, the field looked pretty much the same as it does today.

Play for Pay

The Scottish clubs were particularly admired by the clubs in northern England, just south of the Scottish border. In the early years of the Football Association, these teams often felt like second-class outfits compared to the powerful teams in London.

One way they could play "catch-up" was to take these hardy Scotsmen onto their teams. To lure them down from the north—and to keep them from joining another club—often meant paying these players under the table. And that was against the Football Association's most fundamental rule: All players at that time had to be amateurs.

This skirting of the rules did not present a major problem until 1882, when the Blackburn Rovers made it to the FA Cup final. The Rovers were the first club from the north to make it that far, and they were hardly what one would call a collection of gentlemen. The team was originally made up of former students of the Blackburn Grammar School but now included factory workers, manual laborers, and other "low-class ruffians" (as one paper put it), many of whom had never heard of Blackburn until they were given jobs there in exchange for their services on the soccer pitch. After the game, which Blackburn barely lost, the Association added a rule that threatened to exclude any club paying a player to perform. It was a rule aimed squarely at the northern teams, which routinely abused a regulation permitting clubs to reimburse players for lost wages. Some clubs were known to have paid their stars 100 pounds or more, far more than any worker might have been docked by his employer for missing a few days of work during the course of a year. In the eyes of soccer lovers, this threatened to become a full-blown crisis, especially when the northern clubs threatened to pull out of the Football Association and set up their own league.

It may seem silly today, but professionalism in sports was a very new idea back then—and not a very popular one. The best known pro athletes of the time were prize-fighters and jockeys, who regularly consorted with gamblers and other shady characters. To allow soccer players to play for pay might mean letting this very same element slither into a game that had taken so many centuries to "clean up." As the practice of paying players spread south from clubs in the highlands, the Football Association tried to ignore it, hoping it would go away. It was a naive reaction: What sane person would refuse to be paid for something he was already doing for free? It was also a bit hypocritical. Those who pushed to keep soccer an amateur's game talked of high ideals, of honor and sportsmanship, of the purity of doing something for the camaraderie and sheer enjoyment of it. Yet these were the same men

HEY! I'M OPEN!

Although soccer had been played in one form or another for centuries prior to the late 1800s, it never really occurred to players that they might pass the ball. Even in the early days of the Football Association, soccer was almost exclusively a dribbling game. A player would weave through the defense single-handedly while his teammates looked on. If he made it all the way to the goal, he could score. If the ball was poked away, there was a mad scramble for possession until another player started dribbling it. One of the first soccer stars was R. W. S. Vidal of the Wanderers club, who was hailed as the "Prince of Dribblers." In one famous game, he took the kickoff and dribbled untouched past 10 defenders and scored three consecutive times. In the 1872 FA Cup final between the Wanderers and the Royal Engineers, Vidal stunned the crowd by passing the ball to a wide-open teammate, M. P. Betts, who calmly booted the ball into the Engineers goal for a 1-0 victory. Despite Vidal's moment of inspiration, it would be the Scottish clubs that developed soccer's first real passing game.

IMPERFECT FORM

In the early years of organized soccer, the game on the field could get very disorganized. Most teams sent eight of their players after the ball, keeping a goalie and one other man back on defense, with another man positioned behind the play who could either charge in or retreat back. From this crude formation came the terms fullback (referring to the defender who played fully back) and halfback (referring to the man who played half-way back). In the 1870s, Scottish clubs opened up the game with their long passes, causing defenses to pull another halfback and another fullback off the front line to create a 6-2-2 formation. Not until the 1890s did most teams begin to employ a scheme featuring five forwards, three halfbacks and two fullbacks. From there, a century of tinkering has produced any number of different alignments, including the defense-oriented 2-4-4 used by most teams today.

The kickoff of a game between Germany and Bolivia in the 1994 World Cup. Today, most teams use a defensive 2-4-4 alignment.

who in business aspired to become empire builders through the use of economic might and cutthroat commercial practices.

Finally, when it became clear that nothing short of an investigation was in order, the Association launched one. The suspected pros kept their mouths shut and the offending clubs had their books in order, so nothing could be proved. So outraged at this result were the clubs that had adhered to the amateur rule that several considered leaving the Association in protest.

Midway through the 1883–84 season, the Association came to the conclusion that it had to rethink its position on professionals. When the Upton Park club leveled charges of professionalism at the Preston North End club, the Preston president admitted he paid his players. He also claimed he could prove that every top club in the country did the same! It seemed silly to continue pretending that soccer was an amateur game, especially when the paying public did not seem to care. The 1885 FA Cup saw two "working class" teams compete in the final, and 27,000 people showed up to watch. Shortly thereafter, the Football Association officially legalized professional players.

During its amateur days, soccer was viewed by most as an interesting and amusing pastime. The only people who took it seriously were those who could afford to. The idea of playing soccer instead of working for a living seemed absurd to everyday people. But suddenly, with the acceptance of professionals, the sport presented an opportunity to make an excellent living. A young man looking down the barrel of a life of factory work or hard labor in a mine had a special incentive to improve his dribbling, passing, and shooting skills, whereas a young man of education and means did not. With more than 100 clubs willing to pay for top players, in no time at all soccer passed from the hands of the privileged to the hands of the people. Speeding this process along was a development brought about by Britain's industrial age: the worker's "half-holiday." Each Satur-

day at lunchtime, millions of people who had traditionally worked a six-day week got the rest of the day off. Naturally, many spent this time watching or playing soccer.

The National Sport

At this point, soccer became, for all practical purposes, England's national sport. Kids dreamed of becoming soccer heroes, and fans jammed the local grounds to root for the local team. In 1888, a second soccer organization, the Football League, was formed with 12 clubs. The Football League concentrated on promoting its matches in the newspapers (more people were reading than ever before—another product of Britain's industrial age) and introduced the concept of a regular schedule and a glamorous trophy to ensure high interest in the game. It modeled itself in many ways on the National League, the U.S. baseball organization that paid the country's top players to perform in an elite league, while millions

HATS OFF

In 1886, football associations began awarding honorary "caps" to players who represented their country in international competition. (In the early days, players were actually given hats. Today, no hat is given, and a cap is used as a statistical measurement.) A cap is the equivalent of an appearance or game played, and the term remains in wide use today. As a comparative statistic, a cap is most useful among players for one country, as the same criteria are being used to select players for the international team. Comparing caps for players from different countries, however, can be very misleading. For example, a player with 25 caps for a soccer power, such as Brazil or Italy, is far more impressive than someone with 50 caps for a less-competitive nation, such as Cameroon or Norway.

English star D. R. Gow played in the 1890s. By this time, soccer had become the national sport in England.

continued to play the game on an amateur level. The idea made a lot of sense: why not let the Football Association continue as an amateur organization, while the Football League forged ahead as a pro circuit? By 1898, the Football League boasted 36 teams in two divisions. The League and the Association operated with and against each other, and this sometimes uneasy alliance ushered in the modern era of professional soccer.

Early Stars

The game in the 1890s was not as free-flowing as it is today. Five men played up front as forwards, three played in the middle as halfbacks, and a pair of fullbacks guarded the area in front of the goal. Although players pinched in or moved away from each other as dictated by the course of play, each more or less stayed in his own sector of the field. Given this basic approach, anyone blending above-average skills with a little creativity could, and often did, enjoy tremendous on-field success.

Several stars emerged during these early years. The top halfbacks of this era were Alec Raisbeck and Nudger Needham. Raisbeck was soccer's man in motion, cruising midfield non-stop to thwart attacks before they started and creating breaks the other way. Needham played the left side, where he could be counted upon to stall developments on the opposing right wing. A hard and effective tackler, Needham was known as the "Prince of Halfbacks."

Between the posts, bravery was perhaps the main qualification for stardom in the 1890s. The game often reverted back to its primitive beginnings with wild scuffles in front of the net that produced a great many goals. A keeper crazy enough to throw himself on the ball in these situations was held in great regard. The best goalies of this period, however, were the ones who brought something extra to their position, be it anticipation, leaping ability, or simply a pair of sure hands. What Billy Foulke brought to Sheffield United in 1894 was a massive frame and cat-quick reflexes. Affectionately nicknamed "Fatty," he dwarfed the other players of his era. Yet Foulke had no problem covering the net, especially on low balls, which have always proved difficult for large goalies.

On the wings, Billy Bassett set the standard for outside-rights during the 1890s, threading one perfect pass after another to his West Bromwich teammates. In the 1892 FA Cup semifinal, which was played during a blinding snowstorm, six of Bassett's crosses resulted in goals. Later in the decade, Billy Meredith rose to stardom at this position. With a trademark toothpick jutting from his mouth, he worked the sideline like a magician, pounding the ball inside with well-placed crosses, as well as swooping in himself for spectacular goals. On the opposite

Nottingham Forest captain Ernest "Nudger" Needham poses before a 1913 match against Arsenal.

CUP CAPERS

In 1895, the first FA Cup was stolen from the display window of a shop in Birmingham, England, and never seen again. The World Cup trophy has not fared much better. During World War II, it was hidden under a bed in Italy, and in 1966 it was stolen after being moved to London. A dog named Pickles unearthed it from a hedgerow on the eve of the tournament and became an international hero. After Brazil retired the trophy with its third World Cup win in 1970, it was stolen from its display in Rio de Janeiro and has not turned up since.

Billy Meredith of Manchester United works the touch line during a 1908 match against the Queens Park Rangers.

nation, he could convert a loose ball into a cannon shot without even trapping it. Playing for England in the early "international" matches against Scotland, Wales, and Ireland, Bloomer had Smith feeding him from the left and Bassett passing to him from the right to form a lethal combination.

Early Teams

During the 1890s, the top teams in Great Britain, and thus the best in the world, were the Aston Villa and Sunderland clubs. Aston Villa, led by center-forward John Devey, took the league title five times between 1894 and 1900 and won the FA Cup in 1895 and 1897. The team boasted the fastest halfback in the league, Jimmy Cowan, and an even faster player on the right wing, Charlie Athersmith. When Athersmith and Devey had their two-man game working, they were hard to stop. Nicknamed the "Team of All Talents," Sunderland featured a collection of mainly Scottish-born stars. The club finished first in 1892, 1893, and 1895 and was runner-up in the standings three times between 1894 and 1901. Hugh Wilson was the field general for Sunderland during its glory years. His great anticipation on defense and supreme skill throwing the ball in from the touchline enabled forwards John Campbell and Jimmy Millar to concentrate on scoring, which they did in great abundance. When teams failed to mark Wilson, however, his foot was strong and accurate enough to blow the ball past any goalie in the league. Sunderland's key defender was Jimmy Crabtree, who played both halfback and fullback.

wing was one of the era's great crowd pleasers, Alec Smith. His patented move was to dribble the ball full-out at an opponent, get him backpedaling, and then bust a quick move to leave him in a tangled heap.

The Preston North End club, which completed the first Football League season without a defeat, boasted one of the smartest players in the game in center-forward John Goodall. Rivaling Goodall during the 1890s was G. O. Smith, who did not look the part of a typical center-forward. Frail, thin, and an unfailing gentleman, he put up with constant pounding but used his intelligence and strong right foot to become a deadly finisher. The top inside-forward of his day—and soccer's first true goal-scoring machine—was Steve Bloomer. A supreme opportunist with excellent coordi-

Spreading the Seeds

The latter half of the 19th century saw

STEVE BLOOMER

Soccer's first great scorer was Steve Bloomer, an inside-forward who regularly led the Football League's First Division in goals. One of the rare early players who could blast the ball equally well with either foot, he netted 352 league goals while playing for the Derby County and Middlesbrough clubs in a career that began in the 1890s and lasted more than 20 years. He also scored 28 times in 23 international matches for England. Both of these marks stood up for decades.

Bloomer was not big, and his drawn complexion earned him the nickname "Paleface." Needless to say, he was a natural target for the bruising fullbacks of his era. But Bloomer was quick; he was smart; and his timing was impeccable.

That timing finally failed him in 1914, when he retired as a player to take a job coaching in Berlin, Germany. When World War I erupted a few months later, he was definitely in the wrong place at the wrong time. Bloomer spent the entire war as a prisoner of the Germans.

Remarkably, he did not quit soccer. On the contrary, he organized his own football association at the Ruhleben prisoner-of-war camp and convinced his German captors—many of whom were big soccer fans—to let his fellow prisoners play daily games at a nearby racecourse. After the war, Bloomer returned to Derby to impart his wisdom to the players and was employed by the club to work around the stadium. Happily, he was still there in 1946 when Derby won the FA Cup for the first and only time in the club's long history.

Britain's political influence and economic might touch every corner of the earth. Hundreds of thousands of young men left England in search of fortune, adventure, or just a better life. Some went as soldiers, some went as merchants, some went as students or teachers, and some went as laborers. Some even went as convicts. And with them they brought their game. Soccer was, after all, quite portable. No special equipment was needed to play, and the rules were fairly simple: mark out the boundaries of the field, drive a couple of sticks into the ground at each end, find a ball, and you have a game!

Soccer in something close to its modern form first hit the European continent in the 1860s, when English students at German boarding schools introduced it to their classmates. The first country outside of Great Britain to truly embrace soccer was Denmark, where a football club was formed in 1879. In the succeeding decades, European nations imported English pros to coach their best players. In 1887, Italians learned of soccer from a businessman returning from a trip

THE GOLDEN RULES

During the 1870s, several important rules were put into effect. Corner kicks were awarded to attacking teams when the ball went across the end line off a defending player, and the one-handed throw-in was replaced by the current two-hand rule. To discourage players from deliberately stopping the ball with their hands, the free kick was established, and it quickly became the answer to a number of other infractions. Violent fouls were met with a direct free kick that could result in a score, while minor violations merited indirect free kicks, where the ball had to be touched by another player before a goal could be scored.

In 1882, representatives from the English, Scottish, Irish, and Welsh football associations met in Manchester, England, to eliminate the basic differences in rules and equipment. From this meeting came several key changes, affecting the game's equipment, the field, and the goal. A regulation size for a soccer ball was established, sidelines (or touch lines) were to be clearly marked, and goals had to have crossbars instead of string or tape.

to London. In the mid-1890s, Hungary made tremendous gains in soccer after a couple of Englishmen joined the national team, and in 1899, four British players helped form FC (Football Club) Barcelona in Spain.

The most successful ambassadors of soccer during the 1880s and 1890s were English textile merchants, especially those from the region of Lancashire, from which half of the founding 12 teams of the Football League originated. In 1887, two brothers running a textile mill in the Russian town of Chrekhoro showed the game to their workers. Within a few years, an entire league was in operation in nearby Moscow. The British textile industry was also involved in the introduction of soccer to Iceland, Turkey, Sweden, Rumania, Portugal, and Czechoslovakia (now the Czech Republic and Slovakia).

Soccer gained an especially strong foothold in Austria, where a large population of Englishmen in the capital city of Vienna helped form the First Vienna Football Club and the Vienna Cricket and Football Club. The first game was played there in 1894, and in 1897 the Austrian Football Union was formed. A talented English player and travel agent, M. D. Nicholson, was its first president. A young Austrian named Hugo Meisl found the game utterly enchanting, and over the next few years he helped to spread soccer throughout Europe. Meisl was a key figure behind the creation of the Mitropa Cup and the Nations Cup, two important tournaments in the formative days of soccer.

On the other side of the Atlantic Ocean, soccer arrived in South America in 1874, when British sailors first played the game in Brazil. In 1878, a special match was held for Princess Isabella of Portugal, and interest began to mount. Soccer eventually became Brazil's national passion after Charles Miller, the son of British immigrants, returned to the city of São Paulo after playing professionally for Southampton during a 10-year stay in England. Miller convinced British workers in Brazil to form soccer teams in the 1890s, and by 1898 the sport had become so popular among the locals that they were able to form extremely competitive teams.

In 1891, British railroad workers formed Uruguay's first soccer club, and it eventually became the international power known as Peñarol. English residents of Buenos Aires tried to introduce the game in Argentina at this time, but with less success. The seeds were sown, however, and eventually it was Italian immigrants who helped the sport blossom in the early years of the 20th century. Soccer also prospered in the British colonies in Africa and Asia and had gained footholds in Australia and Canada by the turn of the century.

Soccer in the States

England exported soccer to every corner of the earth during the 19th century. Yet nowhere did it meet with greater initial acceptance than in the sports-mad United States. The game was played in most North American schools and universities during the 1870s and 1880s, and many clubs sprang up in the New York area, where there were high concentrations of English, Irish, and Scottish immigrants. In 1873, four major U.S. universities—Columbia, Princeton, Rutgers, and Yale—asked the nation's most prestigious school, Harvard, to join in something called the Intercollegiate Football Association. At the time, remember, "football" was still a general term meaning rugby or soccer, and when Harvard discovered that the other schools were referring to the "kicking game" and not the "carrying game," it politely refused. Some believe that if Harvard had thrown its considerable weight behind soccer at this time, it might have become our national game, or at least the predominant fall sport. The way it worked out, rugby became the sport of choice, and within a decade it had evolved into the game now known as football.

In the summer of 1884, the American Football Association was formed in Newark, New Jersey, in an attempt to make sense out of a tangled, discordant mess of leagues and teams. Soccer had failed to grow as quickly as other new sports, such as baseball, because the clubs and associations in the United States failed to see the value of working together to help the game grow. Indeed, for two decades, constant bickering,

The Harvard team posed for this 1911 photograph after defeating archrival Yale 3-1. Soccer was played at many colleges and universities as early as the 1870s.

jockeying for power, and petty jealousies kept soccer off the sports pages and largely out of sight.

The AFA immediately began its own version of the FA Cup, which it called the American Cup. Thirteen teams competed for the silver trophy in 1884–85, with the championship going to the O.N.T. club, which was sponsored by Clark Thread Mills. The squabbling continued over the next two decades. Several new leagues formed and then quickly disbanded, but by and large the AFA was able to maintain order.

International competition during the 19th century was primarily limited to matches against Canada. In 1884, a team from Ontario journeyed to St. Louis, where they beat a U.S. team twice. A year later, a group from New York played in Toronto and lost 2-1. This game was doubly noteworthy: It was the first international match ever played in Canada and the first sporting event in that country to be played under artificial lights. The United States's first international victory came in November 1886 when a group of local stars beat the Canadian national team 3-2 on a soggy field in Kearney, New Jersey. U.S.–Canadian competition continued, especially on the club level, throughout the 1880s, and in the summer of 1891, the two countries joined forces and sent a team of all-stars on a five-month, 58-game tour of the British Isles. As expected, they were trounced regularly. The team, which included nine Americans, did manage to win 13 matches and tie 13 more.

Clark Thread Mills' O.N.T. team won the first American Cup championship in 1885.

The 1890s saw tremendous growth in United States soccer. Leagues were formed in the western states of California and Colorado, as well as in such midwestern cities as Cleveland and Cincinnati. In St. Louis, the Kensingtons—a team made up entirely of Native Americans—dominated league play.

During this period, soccer's power base shifted north from the New York–New Jersey area to New England, where clubs from Massachusetts and Rhode Island captured seven consecutive American Cups. The game itself was opening up, too. As had been true of British soccer, during the formative years of the game in the United States a player would dribble the ball up the field with teammates clearing a path before him and protecting his flanks. By the 1890s, however, players were positioned in set areas and worked to get open for a shot or pass. Most U.S. teams employed either a 6-2-2 (six forwards, two halfbacks or midfielders, and two fullbacks protecting the goalie) set-up, or a 5-3-2 "pyramid."

Football with the Feet

The first professional league in the United States came about in 1894. It was the brainchild of baseball owners looking to keep their turnstiles spinning after the season ended, and it was an ambitious undertaking to say the least. The American League of Professional Football Clubs boasted teams in six major cities: Brooklyn, Baltimore, Philadelphia, Boston, New York City, and Washington, D.C. The league scheduled a total of 50 games, with a demanding four-a-week schedule starting in early October. It was strictly no-frills: The home teams wore white uniforms with black socks, while the visitors wore black uniforms with white socks. AFA officials resented the baseball magnates moving into their sport, and they immediately passed a rule stating that anyone signing to play professionally would be banned from the AFA.

Newspapers in the six cities got behind the new league in a big way. Diagrams were printed and rules and strategies were explained so that fans could understand what it was that they were paying to see. Understandably, many were expecting to see the "football" played in colleges and by amateur teams in Pennsylvania and Ohio. The press tried to make the difference clear by referring to soccer as "association" football; the *New York Times* ran a two-column feature entitled "Football With The Feet."

The season opened to small but enthusiastic crowds. A lot of people were seeing soccer for the first time, and they liked it. They cheered lustily when players made sliding tackles and went wild when goals were scored. Fans especially enjoyed it when a player used his head to redirect the ball. Off the field, however, things were not going well. After losing 10-1 to Baltimore, the manager of the Washington team claimed that his opponent was using English pros who, technically, were not allowed to play in the United States. At the same time, British teams were not very happy that several of their players had broken their contracts to come to America and play for higher salaries.

Fearing the Treasury and Immigration Departments might get involved in the dispute, league owners met to discuss the future of their venture. The issue of foreign players was just one of many problems. Another was college football, which was killing weekend attendance. Less than three weeks into the season, the American League of Professional Football Clubs folded.

At first, the failure of the professionals seemed to breathe new life into the amateur game, but by the end of the 19th century, interest in soccer had begun to wane. Football was becoming America's fall sport, and a curious new game called basketball was catching on during the winter months. The American Cup did not make it past 1898, and

Players battle for possession of the ball during a soccer match in Boston. Soccer was initially a great success in the United States, but feuds between rival soccer organizations stunted the sport's growth.

several important soccer clubs disbanded due to lack of enthusiasm and shaky finances. As the 20th century began, soccer in the United States was right back where it had started. Yet in virtually every other part of the world, it was getting ready to explode.

A New Century

The game of soccer in the early years of the 20th century was almost identical to today's game. Rules and strategies have remained largely unchanged during this century; only the equipment, conditions, and style of play have evolved in significant ways. But in those early years, the game was still dominated by Great Britain. The FA Cup was the most prestigious competition in the world, and the best teams in the world were all playing in the British Isles. But potential competitors were springing up all over the globe.

Italians were mad for the game. Between 1900 and 1910, strong clubs were formed in most of the country's major cities, and huge crowds showed up for their games. Soccer took root in Uruguay and Argentina, and the two countries met for the first time in 1901, spurred on by a trophy donated by British tea magnate Sir Thomas Lipton.

In Brazil, soccer started as a more refined game for the upper class. But after humiliating defeats at the hands of visiting Englishmen in 1906 and 1910, working-class Brazilians took up the game themselves as a matter of national pride. A young man named Arthur Friedenreich was Brazil's first great star, as well as an agent of social change. His father was German and his mother a dark-skinned Brazilian. At the time, the sport in Brazil did not welcome young men with dark complexions, but Friedenreich was so good that he left his fellow players little choice. After breaking the country's color line, he went on to obliterate every soccer record in the book, winding up as the first player in the world to net more than 1,000 career goals.

By 1902, Hungarian and Austrian teams played each other for the first time, while France, Belgium, and Holland also began to venture beyond their own borders to play in other countries. The English were proud that their game had taken off so quickly, but by the same token, they could not have been less interested in promoting its international growth. When a meeting of soccer-playing countries was held in Paris in 1904, the English did not even bother to send a delegate!

An International Organization

The problem, as the British saw it, was that they had already been holding their own "international" tournament for two decades by then (albeit limited to England, Ireland, Scotland, and Wales). They thought it rather preposterous that these soccer beginners across the English Channel would think so much of themselves as to form an international body. So the meeting forged ahead without the British, and from it came the Federation Internationale de Football Association (FIFA), which is still soccer's worldwide governing organization.

By 1914, when World War I put soccer on hold, FIFA boasted 23 members, including England, which joined on the condition that its International Board would have total control over the rules of the game. Each country had one vote, although the British effectively had four since England, Scotland, Ireland, and Wales were considered individual members. It was FIFA's task in those early years to ensure that everyone was playing exactly the same game, to resolve disputes regarding international competition, and to share information among its members. The associations representing its member countries were all amateur organizations, as professional soccer outside of England would not develop until the 1920s. Thanks to this atmosphere of friendship and cooperation, FIFA became strong during the years prior to World War I. And this, in turn, enabled soccer to emerge from the

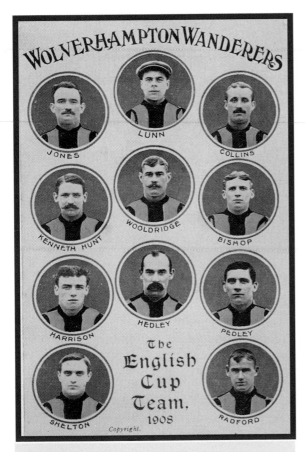

The Wolverhampton Wanderers won the FA Cup in 1908.

This early 20th century postcard depicts a soccer match in the United States.

four-year struggle in perfect position to become the world's most popular sport.

The Olympics

The first international proving ground for soccer would come in the Olympic Games. The first modern Olympics were held in Athens, Greece, in 1896, and it did more to popularize sports in general than it did to put soccer on the map. In fact, there is no record of any games being played, although many who attended the Games remembered a match between a Danish club and a team of Greeks. Then as now, the Summer Games were held every four years, so soccer's next chance came in 1900 at the Paris Olympics. Though not recognized as an official sport, soccer was played by contin-

gents from England, France, and Denmark, making it the first team sport allowed in the Olympics. England, which was represented by the Upton Park club from London, defeated both opponents easily, taking the final 4-0 against a French all-star team.

St. Louis hosted the Olympic Games in 1904. As it turned out, the city was ill-prepared to host the games, and because of this lack of readiness, the Olympics featured some of the weirdest moments in sports history, including a marathon won by an athlete who rode part of the way in an automobile. Almost forgotten in this debacle was soccer. But it was played, and by all accounts played well. The Galt Football Club from Ontario, Canada, shutout two U.S. teams—one made up of railroad workers and the other a group of local students.

MAY I HAVE A TRANSFER, PLEASE?

In 1905, the soccer world was rattled by the news of Alf Common's transfer from the Sunderland football club to Middlesbrough. Common was one of the Football League's most dangerous scorers, but the 1,000 pound fee forked over by his new club was more than double the going rate for a good player. No one was more pleased than Common, who pocketed a small percentage of that money. No one was more enraged than league chairman Charles Clegg, who was convinced that this move would touch off bidding wars that might one day run soccer into the ground. Clegg's anger also stemmed from the fact that, as owner of the Sheffield United club, he had actually sold Common to Sunderland a few months earlier for only 375 pounds. And to cap off Clegg's frustration, Common scored the game-winning goal in his first appearance for Middlesbrough . . . against Sheffield United!

Clegg was right, of course. Despite various attempts to hold down transfer fees—and also the percentage players received as bonuses for switching clubs—the numbers did rise slowly over the next seven decades. Italian hero Pietro Anastasi moved from the Varese club to Juventus in 1968 for more than $1 million, and Dutch great Johan Cruyff transferred from Ajax Amsterdam to the Barcelona club in Spain for more than $2 million in 1973. Since then, transfer fees have skyrocketed to ten times those levels and more, as the megabucks generated by soccer have raised the stakes of winning and losing to dizzying levels.

The kind of trades American sports fans are used to seeing are rare in soccer and always have been. Players are normally moved for cash—even though that money is often put immediately toward a replacement—and players get a small percentage of this fee. Thus, a star who moves often from team to team can make a handsome sum on top of his regular salary. So can a lesser player who is transferred frequently. Indeed, a few enterprising souls have made small fortunes jumping from team to team.

The biggest transfer bargain may have been Alfredo Di Stefano, who was picked up for a mere $70,000 by Real Madrid in the 1950s and developed into one of the greatest players in history. The biggest "What If" scenario would have involved the legendary Pelé, who was never transferred. Reportedly, when the Juventus club offered to purchase his services from Santos, the Brazilian government had Pelé declared a national "resource," and thus he could not be taken from the country!

All three teams were awarded unofficial medals for their participation. Years later, the International Olympic Committee recognized this as the first official soccer competition and awarded the gold, silver, and bronze retroactively.

Lagging Behind

Although organized soccer was at a low ebb in the United States during this period, the game was still played by tens of thousands of athletes from grade school to amateur and semipro teams. After the 1904 Olympics, an amateur squad from England called the Pilgrims made a trip to the United States at the invitation of President Theodore Roosevelt. Led by the renowned Vivian Woodward, this same team had toured Europe and stirred great interest in the sport. They hoped to do the same in North America. What they found was plenty of talent but little in the way of teamwork and technique, although the U.S. clubs did manage to win 2 of 23 games against the Pilgrims. One of the country's biggest proponents of soccer, Roosevelt believed that football was too dangerous and even moved to ban the sport. He invited the two brightest Pilgrim stars, Woodward and Fred Milne, to the White House.

The formation of FIFA, along with Roosevelt's support for the sport, gave U.S. soccer a much-needed boost. In 1905, the AFA got going again and Harvard—then a major power in college sports—joined the Intercollegiate Association Football League. In the years prior to World War I, another British squad, the Corinthians, made two tours of the United States, and the Pilgrims returned in 1909.

The two American teams that managed to hold their own against the English were Haverford College and the Fall River Rovers from Quincy, Massachusetts. Clearly, U.S. soccer was ready to be recognized by FIFA, but political squabbles prevented the creation of one national association that represented all of American soccer until 1913, when the United States Football Association (USFA) was formed. The USFA instituted the National Challenge Cup, which—like Britain's FA Cup—was open to both amateurs and pros. The New York Football Association made use of the huge and diverse immigrant population in the New York metropolitan area and began the very popular International Cup competition, with proceeds from the tournament going to injured players. Each team was made up of local players who represented their countries of origin.

The most ambitious soccer program, however, was the brainchild of Bethlehem Steel magnate Charles M. Schwab. He spent a small fortune building a world-class soccer facility and then went out and hired the country's top players, including Neil Clarke, James Ford, James Campbell and Robert Millar, who scored 54 goals in 33 games one season. Not surprisingly, Bethlehem won the Challenge Cup four times between 1915 and 1919.

An International Championship

Most historians regard the 1908 Olympics in London as the first true international championship. FIFA, four years old by this time, was able to convince the IOC that soccer deserved to be an official sport. Six teams from five countries competed, with

The Bethlehem Steel Company won the U.S. national championship in 1918.

England beating Denmark 2-0 in the final to win the gold medal. In 1912, eleven countries sent teams to Stockholm, Sweden. As expected, England won the gold again, beating Denmark 4-2. The 1916 Olympics were canceled because of the war, which ended in 1918. During the pre-war years, the game in South America and Europe developed rapidly, thanks in part to the many retired British stars who accepted handsome salaries to teach abroad.

The Football League claimed a monopoly on the world's top players and teams between 1900 and 1914. The best club in the early days of the 20th century was Newcastle United, which finished first in the league three times between 1905 and 1909 and reached the FA Cup final five times in a seven-year period. Though a frequent upset victim, Newcastle was nonetheless a balanced and powerful squad. There were no superstars on this team, but among the

standouts were halfback Colin Veitch and center forward Albert Shepherd.

Another of the top Football League teams was Manchester United. Halfback Charlie Roberts captained this club, and he was flanked by Dick Duckworth and Alec Bell. These three worked wonders together. Roberts was a tall, graceful player whose supremacy at center-half went largely unchallenged during the prewar era. He did everything well, both on and off the field, setting up scorers Alec Turnbull, Enoch West, and old-timer Billy Meredith, as well as leading the Players Union in its early days. The burly Duckworth, at right-half, presented opponents with the human equivalent of a brick wall. On the left, Bell was a heady, finesse player. This trio was the heart of the team during its league title runs in 1908 and 1911.

The Blackburn Rovers won a pair of league championships in 1912 and 1914.

England pushes the attack against Denmark in the 1908 Olympics soccer finals. The English won the game 2-0 and the gold medal.

The club was led by fullback Bob Crompton, who doubled as the on-field leader of England's international team. Aston Villa remained strong, winning the league title in 1910 and placing second four times between 1908 and 1914. Villa's fortunes hinged on the lethal combination of Joe Bache and Harry Hampton. Bache was the clever setup man, while Hampton's job was to hammer the ball home. This pair led the club to the FA Cup in 1913, with the help of halfbacks Tom Barber and Jim Harrop. In the final, Harrop held Sunderland scoreless during a 20-minute stint in goal after Sam Hardy, the top keeper of the time, left the game with an injury.

The War Years

When war broke out in Europe prior to the 1914–15 season, many of the game's best players swapped their club colors for uniforms. The soccer season went on as scheduled in England, based on the belief that the Germans would receive a quick thrashing and everything would return to normal. But as the months passed and thousands died every day in the conflict, it became clear that soccer would have to be put on hold. The 1915 FA Cup final was attended by 50,000 spectators—most of them soldiers on leave or recuperating from war injuries—and was dubbed the Khaki Cup. From 1915 to 1919, soccer ground to a halt in most of the world. In England, league schedules were halted altogether. In Scotland, Wales, and Ireland, the league played on a limited basis, scheduling games on weekends and holidays so as not to draw fans away from the factory jobs so vital to the war effort. All international matches were canceled between 1915 and 1918.

The most notable club of the war years was Glasgow Celtic, which dominated the Scottish league so completely that some fans complained that they were not doing their best to support the war effort. There was no draft in Great Britain, so soccer players did not technically have to go to war, but they were not allowed to earn their living from soccer, either. Those who did not go to Europe had to work in the shipyards, in factories, and in the mines. In truth, Celtic players did their fair share in the war effort; their amazing 62-game unbeaten streak was simply a testimony to their skill.

With the people of Europe and North America embroiled in war, no one really noticed the great strides being made by soccer in South America. During these years, the game underwent a quiet transformation, becoming a quick, crisp-passing affair that better suited the small physiques and great speed of the men playing at the highest levels in such countries as Uruguay, Brazil, and Argentina.

Going Global

When World War I ended in the fall of 1918, soccer picked up right where it left off in most parts of the world. Although teams were decimated and fields were in disrepair, the thought of getting back to playing the game was so appealing that sheer will overcame just about any obstacle. And with so many people having seen so much of the world, it was only natural that the thoughts of soccer fans were more focused on international competition than ever before.

When the Olympic Games resumed in 1920, England, France, and Belgium—still angry at Germany and its allies—demanded that Germany and its allies be excluded from FIFA. The organization voted down this resolution, insisting that real-life politics had no place in soccer if it was to become a truly international sport. France and Belgium reconsidered their position and stayed with FIFA, but England did not, marking the beginning of a 20-year period during which English soccer and FIFA rarely saw eye to eye. As it turned out, England did enter the 1920 Olympics, but it fielded a skeleton team that was eliminated in the first round by Norway.

Without England as a gold-medal certainty, the games, which were held in Antwerp, Belgium, were wide open. Belgium and a powerful team from Czechoslovakia reached the final. After giving up a pair of goals, the Czechs began to wither under the constant noise produced by 40,000 enemy fans. After one of Czechoslovakia's key players was ejected in the first half, the team walked off the field in protest against referee John Lewis. The IOC awarded the gold to Belgium and ordered a playoff for second place between the French and Dutch teams. But many of the French players had already gone home, so France refused. As a result, Spain, Sweden, and Italy competed in a new round of matches to see who played Holland for the silver medal. The whole affair bordered on the absurd, albeit in the name of fairness and good sportsmanship. Eventually, Spain took the silver medal and Holland settled for bronze.

The 1924 Olympics in Paris represented a major turning point for soccer. The Summer Games were meant to be contested by amateurs, and that rule definitely went for soccer players. The British had long been able to field a crack squad of unpaid players, and up until the 1920s no other country had a professional league. So the issue of who could play or could not had little bearing on Olympic soccer. But by 1924, several nations had paid players, and professional leagues were beginning to form all over the globe. FIFA knew it was in the best interest of soccer to keep the quality of play in the Olympics as high as possible, so it struck a special deal with the IOC to ensure that the top players from each country would be allowed to compete. The English, who were justly proud of their own ability to keep amateurs and pros separate, found this compromise appalling. They pulled out of FIFA altogether and did not bother to send a team to Paris.

In retrospect, it was too bad England did not field an Olympic team in 1924, for it would have provided a suitable opponent for an altogether startling team from, of all places, Uruguay. Never before had a South American country sent a soccer team to the Olympics; never before had European fans seen soccer played this way. The quick, crisp play of the Uruguayans left the Parisian crowds in slack-jawed awe. Everyone had been copying the English all these years, but it was the South Americans who seemed to be playing on an utterly new level. Uruguay was the talk of the town, and in a matter of days the team's flashy halfback, José Andrade, had become the game's most admired international star. More than 50,000 fans paid their way into the final, which saw Uruguay blank Switzerland by a score of 3-0.

The British viewed Olympic soccer with a bit of disdain. After all, with the exception of Andrade, weren't all of the world's top players still on the other side of the English Channel? Indeed they were.

Chief among them was Scotland's Alan Morton, the pesky left wing for the Rangers club of Glasgow. Nicknamed the Wee Blue Devil for his eye-popping dribbling skills and deceptively quick shot, Morton won nine Scottish league championships with the Rangers and established himself as the top player of the early 1920s.

The best manager of the day was Herbert Chapman, who took the Huddersfield Town club from obscurity to a pair of league championships and an FA Cup. A molder of young stars with a genius for plucking promising players off the rosters of other teams, Chapman built the foundation of a dominant club before taking the head job with Arsenal in 1925. Huddersfield kept rolling after his departure, winning a third straight league title in 1926 and finishing second in 1927 and 1928.

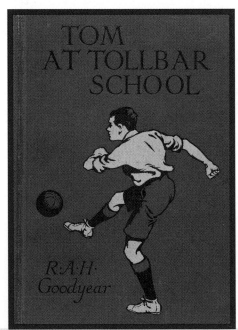

The cover of this 1920s English novel, *Tom at Tollbar School*, shows soccer's importance in young-adult literature.

GETTING IN GEAR

One of the reasons soccer is called the "simplest game" is because there are only two pieces of equipment that really matter: shoes and balls. In the sport's early days, players would fashion studs out of leather and then nail them to their ankle-high workboots. This basic design remained the same until the late 1950s, when adidas introduced a high-quality leather shoe with special screw-in studs.

As for the ball, for more than a century it was made of hand-stitched, brown leather panels, and it absorbed enough moisture in a typical game to make heading it a brain-rattling experience. After World War II, high-grade leather was so hard to come by that balls often burst during games. White balls first came into use in the 1950s, but the traditional brown models were still in play until the 1970s. Today's balls are actually slightly heavier than the old-time models but do not soak up water during a match and are much easier on the eyes and the head.

The soccer ball has gone through many changes over the years. Today's balls are made of high-grade leather.

A Whole New Ball Game

In 1925, a seemingly minor rules change in soccer changed the game forever. During the early 1920s, matches with 30, 40, and 50 offside calls were not uncommon, and it was beginning to drive fans crazy. The offside rule at the time stated that an offensive player could not receive the ball unless there were two defenders and a goalie in front of him. Taking gross advantage of this rule, Newcastle fullbacks Bill McCracken and Frank Hudspeth had perfected a trick where one would play up at midfield and then sneak behind the opposing lead forward when the ball changed possession.

That left the other team with no one to pass to as they started upfield. It got so bad that visiting players would hop off the train at the Newcastle station and joke "Blimey, offside already!" when the conductor blew his whistle.

In June 1925, the International Board decided that it was no longer necessary for an offensive player to keep two defenders between himself and the goalie. Now only one was required. The results were spectacular. On opening day of the 1925–26 season, Aston Villa scored 10 times versus Burnley, and Newcastle beat Arsenal 7-0. That season, Bobby Skinner obliterated the British scoring record with 53 goals for Dunfermline. And by season's end, there were

Bill "Dixie" Dean holds an old-time laced soccer ball. The popular English player was one of soccer's most prolific scorers.

DIXIE DEAN

DIXIE DEAN

In the late 1920s, the United States was experiencing its golden age of sports, with such immortals as Babe Ruth, Red Grange, Bill Tilden, and Jack Dempsey fighting one another for headlines. England had its own superstar, and his exploits on the soccer pitch were every bit as exciting as those luminaries on the other side of the Atlantic. His name was Bill Dean, but everyone called him "Dixie." He was young and handsome, with a magnetic personality and—like the mighty Babe—he possessed a set of skills that were absolutely ideal to take advantage of the dramatic changes his sport was undergoing.

Dean was just 20 years old when he played his first international matches for England in 1927, scoring 12 goals in five games to take the nation's breath away. The offside rule had recently been changed, giving aggressive forwards many more scoring opportunities than in the past. Dean was aggressive all right, but he was highly skilled in other key areas. He was strong yet supple, with wonderful timing and great body control. He could turn on a burst of speed or stop on a dime and launch a searing shot with either foot. From his position at center-forward for the Everton club, Dean also had ample opportunities to go after balls in traffic, and this he did seemingly without regard for his own welfare. Beyond Dean's skills were his marvelous leadership qualities. Rarely if ever did he lose his composure, despite every dirty trick the defenders attempted.

When it came to heading the ball, Dean—who had an awesome vertical leap—was at his best. This was no small matter, considering the weight of a damp soccer ball in those days and the fact that Dean had fractured his skull in a 1926 motorcycle accident. The silver plates that were fastened to his skull only added to his aura in the eyes of his adoring fans. In point of fact, more than half of Dean's goals came while he was in midair, either on perfectly placed headers or on wheeling blasts that sometimes saw his body parallel to the turf as foot met ball. During the 1927–28 league season he hammered a record 60 goals into the net to break the one-year-old mark set by George Camsell. As always, Dean accomplished this feat with the utmost dramatic flair, reeling off no fewer than nine goals in his final three games.

What a season that was! His 60 goals in 39 games is still an English record, as are the seven hat tricks he recorded that year. He scored another 22 in various international and cup games, too, bringing his grand total that year to 82. Dean continued to score even though defenses tightened up during the 1930s, finishing with 349 goals in 399 league matches. Injuries ended his career prematurely in 1939.

6,373 goals scored in the league as opposed to just 4,700 the year before.

Sensing what would happen before the season even started, Charlie Buchan of Arsenal begged manager Herbert Chapman to try a new alignment. He believed the center-halfback, usually an attacker in the standard 2-3-5 alignment, should come back and play defense between the two full-backs. One of the inside-forwards would then move to the middle on the attack to create a 3-3-4 formation. Chapman ignored Buchan until they were blown out 7-0 in the opener, then gave in. The next game they shutout West Ham 4-0. Many feel this event marked the birth of modern soccer. Over the next three decades, almost every team in the world adopted some variation of this setup, and slowly but surely, soccer evolved into the defensive-minded game it is today.

In the short run, however, the scoring binge continued as defenses struggled to adjust to the new rule. In 1926–27 Middlesbrough center-forward George Camsell booted 59 goals in 37 games, and a year later 21-year-old center-forward Dixie Dean of Everton scored 60. Goal 60 came on a header with just 8 minutes left in the final game and made Dean a national hero. Similar scenarios played out all over the world, as the new offside rule was adopted by virtually every soccer-playing country.

Stars of the Twenties

With the game's focus suddenly on scoring, fans focused more than ever on scorers and talented set-up men. During the late-1920s, a new crop of stars arrived, and for the first time they were not all British. Among the more compelling young players was Giuseppe Meazza, who shattered the Italian league record with 33 goals for the Internazionale club as an 18-year-old in 1928–29. Another was Ivan Bek of Yugoslavia, who scored 51 goals in 50 games for Belgrade in 1926–27. One of the first players to leave his country to play professionally in a foreign league, Bek transferred to FC Sète in France and eventually adopted that country as his home.

The Abegglen brothers, from Switzerland, also had a knack for finding the net. Max Abegglen had led all Olympic scorers in 1924 and increased his goal-getting prowess in the late-1920s after the offside rule was changed. His brother Trello, however, emerged as the better of the two. He led the Zurich Grasshoppers to a pair of league championships and played brilliantly at inside-forward for the Swiss team during international matches.

In Belgium, Raymond Braine distinguished himself as that country's most proficient player, starring for the Beerschot club during the 1920s before moving to the high-powered Sparta club in Prague, Czechoslovakia. He was so good in that league that he was asked to become a Czech citizen.

In England, where the scoring feats of Camsell and Dean grabbed many of the headlines, Alex James of Manchester United developed into the finest playmaking inside-forward of his time. A rough, no-holds-barred player when he started, James rechanneled his devilish impulses and became a master at creating goals with impossible passes. His goal-scoring figures may not have been impressive, but he was one of the most popular players in soccer for more than a decade.

Between the Posts

With great offense, there inevitably developed great defense, or, more to the point, great goalies. Once a relatively quiet profession, goalkeepers were now quite literally on the firing line. The onslaught was continuous, with play racing up and down the field at a breakneck pace. The fans loved it, but many netminders crumbled under the constant pressure. Those who thrived under these circumstances quickly earned international reputations. The most well-known were Ricardo Zamora of Spain, Gianpiero Combi of Italy, and Czech star Frantisek Planicka. All three proved they could come up with the big save and bounce back from injuries and adversity.

The 1928 Olympics

Because so many of these talented players were performing in professional leagues,

Uruguay defeated Argentina 2-1 to win the gold medal in soccer at the 1928 Summer Olympics.

they would not be allowed to compete in the 1928 Olympics. After bending the rules a bit in 1924, the IOC came down firmly against the inclusion of professionals on Olympic soccer teams. Still, some of the world's top players did appear. Midfield genius José Nasazzi starred for Uruguay, showing why his countrymen called him "The Marshall," as he stopped enemy advances and spurred his own troops back up the field. Argentina claimed two top players in super-aggressive center-half Luisito Monti and crafty left winger Raimondo Orsi. These two countries disposed of their European challengers with ease and eventually met in the final, a 1-1 deadlock that ended in darkness. They played it again the next day, and Uruguay triumphed 2-1.

The all-South American final had two important consequences for the history of soccer. First, it drove home a point first made in 1924: the European way of playing was neither the only way nor necessarily the best way. Second, the absence of Great Britain and the best professional players from other European countries convinced FIFA that it needed to put on its own tournament. Soccer could still be showcased in the Olympics as an amateur sport, but in between there needed to be a clash of the world's best players regardless of their status.

The First World Cup

At FIFA's 1928 meeting, its two dynamic leaders, President Jules Rimet and Secretary Henri Delaunay, put their idea of a "World Cup" to a vote. It passed 25-5, and preparations for the inaugural tournament in 1930 began. At first, everyone assumed that it would be held somewhere in Europe. But then Uruguay's representatives made an offer that Rimet could not refuse. Uruguay, which was to celebrate its 100th year of independence in 1930, wished to host the first World Cup and was willing to pay the expenses of every team that wished to compete. They also promised to construct a 100,000-seat stadium in the capital city of Montevideo. Many of FIFA's member countries were strapped for cash, so the Uruguayan offer seemed like the perfect solution.

FIFA accepted Uruguay's generous offer to hold the 1930 World Cup, but it did not anticipate the consequences. Holland, Italy, Spain, and Sweden had also offered to play host, and when they learned that Uruguay was to be the venue, they decided not to send their teams. The fact that Uruguay would foot the bill and that the country had twice traveled to Europe to compete in the Olympics carried little weight.

The British withdrawal from FIFA presented another problem. The Football Association, which was still controlled by the amateurs, did not like the idea of sending a team of its best players to compete in an international championship, especially if its best players were all professionals. Also begging out of the World Cup were Hungary and Austria, who figured to give the Uruguayans a run for their money. These countries claimed that the World Cup matches, plus the round-trip ocean voyage, would deprive their professional teams of important players for two months or more. It took some major arm-twisting by Rimet and others, but eventually five European teams made the trip to Montevideo: Belgium, France, Rumania, Yugoslavia, and Hungary.

Representing the Americas were Uruguay, Argentina, Brazil, Chile, Mexico, Paraguay, Peru, and the United States. The 13 teams were divided into three groups of three and one of four, with the group winners to advance to a semifinal round. As expected, Argentina, Uruguay, and Yugoslavia won their groups, but the fourth semifinalist was something of a surprise. The United States fielded players of such immense size and strength that their relative lack of skill hardly mattered. They literally rolled over Paraguay and Belgium, posting a pair of 3-0

TAKE THAT!

As preparations for the first World Cup got under way, the first real hint that the world was catching up to England came in May 1929, when they lost to Spain 4-3 in Madrid. Having played two matches in the previous five days—and without Camsell and Dean—leg-weary England was ambushed early by a team coached by Billy Pentland, an Englishman who played for Middlesbrough earlier in the decade. Spain scored two quick goals, but England tied the score at halftime and grabbed a 3-2 lead early in the second half. But Ricardo Zamora, the world's top goalie, kept them out of the net the rest of the game, and Spain scored the final two tallies.

The U.S. team (in white) battles the Belgium national team during a 1930 World Cup game. The U.S. team prevailed, winning its first World Cup match.

victories. In the semis, however, Argentina drubbed the United States. Uruguay did likewise to Yugoslavia, setting up a dream final between neighboring countries.

Tens of thousands of Argentine fans poured across the Río de la Plata from nearby Buenos Aires and made their way toward the stadium, which had not been completely finished in time for the competition. There they watched their team take a 2-1 lead before Uruguay came storming back with a trio of second-half goals to nail down a 4-2 win. A non-stop party followed in the streets of Montevideo, and each of the Uruguayan players was given a new home in appreciation of the great victory. Meanwhile, in Buenos Aires, Argentine fans pelted the Uruguayan embassy with bottles, stones, and anything else they could lay their hands on.

Aside from some curious refereeing, the first World Cup was a success. It had featured some dramatic moments, overall excellence in play, and it had even turned a profit. More importantly, by staging it in such a far-flung locale, FIFA had convinced Europe's soccer powers that it could be an even grander event on their own home turf.

Stars of the Thirties

During the 1930s the world finally sat up and took notice of the fine brand of soccer being played in South America. Monti and Orsi were imported to Italy and became the heart of the powerful Juventus club, which won the Italian championship five straight times, and several other South Americans came over to Europe during this period. Many players chose to stay home, earning a little less money but a lot more glory, in more comfortable surroundings.

Brazil produced a pair of superstars during the 1930s. Domingos da Guia developed a reputation as the top defensive player on the entire continent while playing professionally in Brazil, Uruguay, and Argentina. Nicknamed the "Divine Master," he had an eerie ability to read the field and thwart opposing attacks before they got started. Leonidas Da Silva, better known as the "Black Diamond," invented the bicycle kick and starred for Brazil in 23 international matches during the decade. He did most of his professional playing for the Nacional club in Uruguay.

In Argentina, Bernabe Ferreyra developed into his country's first pro superstar. Called "The Mortar" for his scoring prowess, he smashed the Argentine league record with 43 goals in 1932–33 and kicked with such velocity and expert placement that a newspaper once offered a gold medal to any goalie who could stop him from point-blank range. Ferreyra retired while still in his prime, which only added to his legend. Another South American who played for just a few years was Paraguay's Arsenio Erico. During his career with the Independente club of Argentina he established himself as one of the game's most dangerous center-forwards, breaking the league record for goals with 47 and inspiring a generation of South American boys who would put the continent permanently on the soccer map two decades later.

Despite the growth of the sport worldwide, the center of the soccer world was still Great Britain, and among the top players to come along during the 1930s were Arsenal teammates Eddie Hapgood and Cliff Bastin. Hapgood spent his entire pro career with Arsenal, where he came up with Herbert Chapman and went on to win five league championships and play in three FA Cup finals. Hapgood was a gritty little player who earned the respect of teammates and opponents alike by making big plays when he had to, even when severely injured—an especially important virtue in the days when substituting was not legal. He also served as captain for England in 21 international matches. Bastin ranked among the top left wings in soccer between the wars, attaining world-class status in his early twenties. He specialized in producing rocket shots from the perimeter, but when asked to move to inside-forward he exhibited the finesse required by that position without a noticeable drop in the quality of his play.

Scotland boasted the decade's most prolific scorer in Jimmy McGrory of the Celtic club. Although his international experience was limited to just seven matches, his league record showed 410 goals in 408 games, making him the only British player ever to average better than a goal a game.

Uruguay's national team poses after winning the 1930 World Cup before a home crowd.

RAIMONDO ORSI

The soccer revolution that ignited in South America during the 1920s came not from one player but from the style of play favored throughout the continent. While the Europeans liked to rely on brute force and raw power to maintain control of their games, players in Uruguay, Brazil, and Argentina focused more on passing, dribbling, and carefully timed bursts of speed. The player who, more than anyone, introduced this style to Europe was Raimondo Orsi.

Born in Argentina in 1901, he was the son of an Italian businessman who had moved his family to Buenos Aires to open a leather factory. Orsi made the national team as a teenager in 1920 and was the best player in South America by the time he transferred to Italy's powerful Juventus club, which he did after starring in the 1928 Olympics.

During his time in Europe, Orsi was the biggest drawing card in the Italian league. And he was paid handsomely by the standards of his day—his 8,000 lira monthly salary was the equivalent to that of a field marshal in the army, and he was a personal favorite of dictator Benito Mussolini, especially after he popped Portugal for a pair of goals in his first appearance with the Italian team in 1929.

Orsi was a sensation, leading the Juventus club to league championships each year from 1931 to 1935. And he was the big hero in the 1934 World Cup final, when he scored a goal that is still talked about in awe. With Italy down 1-0 to Czechoslovakia late in the game, Orsi got the ball on the left wing, faked the defense with his left foot, and then produced a weird shot with his right that went over and then dipped behind the goalkeeper and found its way into the net. The match went into extra time and Italy won. The next day, at the request of reporters, Orsi returned to the field to show them how he had done it. After 20 unsuccessful attempts, he gave up. It was a once-in-a-lifetime shot, and he knew it.

For almost his entire career, Orsi was the fastest man on the field, wherever he played and whomever he played against. How he used this speed, however, was ultimately what defined his greatness. Orsi did not simply outrun his opponents, he used their fear of his speed to gain advantages in other areas where he excelled. He could shoot, pass, and dribble, and he did so with adoring chants of *"Mumo! Mumo!"* cascading down from the stands. Hugo Meisl, whose Austrian "Wunderteam" was arguably the best between the wars, would have given anything to get Orsi on his club and once described him as "the Paganini of football." (Niccolò Paganini was an extraordinarily talented violinist.)

This ball was autographed by members of the Bolton Wanderers in 1929 after they won the FA Cup. Until the 1930s, the English professional leagues were considered far superior to those in other countries.

GOOD NEWS, BAD NEWS

As professional soccer leagues began to develop in most countries, the accepted format of competition came from Great Britain, where a system of "promotion and relegation" had been operating very successfully for decades. To sort out the dozens of clubs competing for a national title, a first division of the most powerful clubs was established. Below that was a second and sometimes even a third division. These were not leagues, however. Any team could join the first division if it played well enough. At season's end, the top one or two clubs from the second division would earn promotion to the first division, while the bottom clubs in the first division would be relegated to the second division. This created excitement and interest in second division matches and generated fierce competition among the bottom-rung teams in the first division.

The United States plays host team Italy in World Cup '34. The Italians won 7-1 and went on to win the World Cup, defeating Czechoslovakia in the final.

World Cup '34

Italy won the chance to host the 1934 World Cup, and dictator Benito Mussolini aimed to make the most of it. For a decade, he had tried to reawaken a sense of Roman history and achievement in his people, and a huge sporting event seemed like a great opportunity to show the world that Italy had returned to its former glory.

The Italian national team was one of the finest in Europe. To further tip the scales in his favor, manager Vittorio Pozzo added several top Argentine players to his squad. These players, like many Argentines, claimed Italian heritage. In fact, hundreds of

Argentines were fighting with the Italian Army in their war with Ethiopia. "If they can die for Italy," proclaimed Pozzo, "they can play football for Italy." With the "home field" advantage—and with the English again out of the World Cup picture thanks to its continued boycott of FIFA—it seemed only Austria stood between Italy and the cup.

The Austrians, however, were something to behold. Nicknamed "Der Wunderteam," they were practically unbeatable. In 1931 and 1932, they embarrassed Scotland, Hungary, Germany, and Switzerland in international matches, rolling up a combined score of 27-3. Their star attacker and spiritual leader was center-forward Matthias Sindelar, who was dubbed the "Man of Paper" for his skinny build. Sindelar was one of the Austrian players who scored in an unlucky 4-3 loss to the all-powerful English in a game that many felt proved that there was little if any difference in quality between the Austrians' play and the play of the team that was considered the best in the world.

World Cup '34 featured 32 teams from all over the globe. Besides the absence of the British, the only noteworthy no-show in 1934 was Uruguay, which decided to return Italy's snub from four years earlier. Everyone was waiting for the inevitable showdown between Italy and Austria which, because of the groupings, would come in the semifinal. When it did come, the weather was horrible and the field was in bad condition. This hurt the Austrians, who featured a complex passing attack, and who had lost a key player, Johann Horvath, to injury. Italy scored the game's lone goal after Austria's keeper lost the ball on a controversial collision with an Italian player and another Italian booted it into the net.

In the final, Italy took on Czechoslovakia, which had established itself as a formidable contender by beating England in a non-World Cup match just prior to the competition. The final was a tough, grueling match controlled by the visitors until, with 10 minutes left, a bizarre, twisting shot from Orsi on the left wing eluded the Czech goaltender and tied the score. The Italians sprang to life in overtime and netted the deciding goal. For the second time, the host team won the World Cup.

World Cup '34 established the reputations of several top international players. Over the next few years, several more European stars came to the fore, including Severino Minelli, Oldrich Nejedly, Gyorgy Sarosi, Bimbo Binder, and Giovanni Ferrari. One of the supreme tacticians of the 1930s, Minelli played a role in six Swiss league championships. Minelli and Karl Rappan lifted Switzerland to victory many times in international play, helping to perfect the "bolt" system that featured an early version of the sweeper back, who swooped in back of the fullbacks on defense as a last line of defense. Nejedly was an inside-left for the great Sparta Prague clubs of the 1930s. He and left wing Antonin Puc worked their magic against opponents for most of the decade. Nejedly scored five times in Czechoslovakia's remarkable World Cup run in 1934, and only a broken leg kept him from starring again in 1938. In Sarosi, Hungary could have laid claim to the best all-around player during the mid-1930s. He led the Ferencvaros club to the

The Italian team celebrates its victory in the 1934 World Cup finals by lifting manager Vittorio Pozzo in the air.

IN DER FÜHRER'S FACE

So successful was the first World Cup in 1930 that the International Olympic Committee (IOC) decided to drop soccer from the 1932 Olympics in Los Angeles. Soccer was restored as an Olympic sport in 1936, partly because the IOC needed the money generated by the huge attendance, and partly at the demand of German dictator Adolph Hitler, who was sure his team would win the gold medal. Among the many public embarrassments suffered by der Führer at the 1936 Olympics was his team's 2-0 loss to Norway, which eliminated Germany from the tournament. Hitler never attended another soccer game in his life.

Hungarian championship nine times during his great career, moving easily between the center-forward and center-half positions. Sarosi blasted 349 goals in 383 games in Hungary and added another 42 in 75 international appearances. Binder was soccer's most prolific scorer during the 1930s, netting more than 1,000 goals in less than 800 games. He anchored the Rapid club of Vienna both before and after Austria was annexed by the Nazis in 1938 and struck a blow for Austrians everywhere when he scored a hat trick against the powerful Schalke club in the Greater German championship of 1941. As for Ferrari, he turned out to be one of only two players to appear for Italy in World Cup '34 and '38. He manned the inside-left position for the national team, as well as for Juventus, which captured five Italian league titles while he was there.

World Cup '38

Needless to say, a number of countries were very keen on hosting World Cup '38. And with the popularity of soccer at an all-time high in Europe, there was much lobbying to keep the tournament from moving back to South America, as originally planned. In the end, FIFA president Jules Rimet decided to bring the World Cup to his home country, France. At the time, cycling and rugby competed with soccer for the French franc, and it was a personal goal of Rimet's to make his game the national passion. That would be up to the talented, but underachieving, French national team.

As the tournament began, however, all was not well in the soccer world, and there were some noticeable absences from the anticipated strong field. In the years between 1934 and 1938, the planet's political situation had grown very dim. A civil war in Spain had all but put soccer on hold in that country, and Austria and its players had been consumed by Germany shortly after the team qualified for a World Cup berth. The English were invited to replace Austria but declined, preferring once again to sit out the World Cup. Asia sent its first representative, the Dutch East Indies team, which qualified automatically after the pullout of Japan, which was too busy invading China to bother with soccer. Argentina decided not to send a team after France was announced as the venue, stating that Rimet had reneged on his promise to alternate sites between the Americas and Europe. That left Cuba and Brazil as the western hemisphere's lone representatives.

So for a variety of reasons having little to do with soccer, World Cup '38 did not feature a particularly strong group of teams. Italy, which had won 22 of 23 international matches since World Cup '34, was the overwhelming favorite to repeat as champions. Ferrari and Meazza returned from the 1934 team, along with several members of the gold-medal Olympic squad of 1936. It even included Uruguayan star Michele Andreolo. As it turned out, the Italians had a little extra incentive to repeat as cup champs. The night before the opening game, the team received a telegram from Mussolini that was short and to the point: "Win or die."

The early matches provided plenty of surprises. Italy barely squeaked past Nor-way, and Switzerland's defense befuddled the Germans, who found it was no easy task to blend the stylish Austrians into their rigid offensive system. What got everyone talking, however, was the performance of Brazil's Leonidas Da Silva. In the opener against Poland he cut the defense to ribbons, scoring three first-half goals. In the second half, with Poland up a goal and the field turned into a quagmire by a sudden rainstorm, Da Silva's shoe stuck in the mud at a crucial moment near the Polish goal. He calmly pulled his foot out of the shoe and blasted a shot into the back of the net with his stocking foot.

The rest of the tournament followed form. Da Silva continued to score goals for Brazil, and Italy continued to win, with center-forward Silvio Piola establishing himself as the star of the team. Piola's fifth and final goal of the World Cup, against Hungary, nailed down the championship. The Italian players had done one of the hardest things in sports: they won when they were supposed

The victorious Italian team holds up the 1938 World Cup trophy after their 4-2 win over Hungary in Paris.

to. And they did so in the face of a death threat from their own national leader, as well as constant jeering from the French crowd, which included many Italians who had been forced to flee their country in the face of fascism. Adding to the overall tension was the fact that most of the participating countries had already chosen sides for what seemed the inevitability of war. Indeed, most of these young men would soon trade their soccer boots for rifles.

Making Strides

The period between 1919 and 1938 was an important one for American soccer. During World War I, the first official U.S. international squad crossed the Atlantic to play a series of matches with teams in neutral countries Norway and Sweden. They did well, going 3-2-1 against various all-star teams, and found time to play a couple of exhibition baseball games for Sweden's King Gustav V, a great lover of sports. So impressed was the king that he ordered Stockholm's schools to teach baseball the following year.

Confident that American players could compete against and beat European teams, U.S. soccer officials were anxious to send another team abroad. In 1919, Charles Schwab beefed up his already dominant Bethlehem club with stars from other teams and sent them off to Scandinavia. In 14 games against Sweden, Finland, Norway, and Denmark, they scored 22 goals, allowed

The Chicago Sparta soccer team was one of the many industrial teams that flourished in the United States in the 1920s. Soccer in the United States made great strides between the two world wars.

15, and posted an impressive 6-2-6 record. In 1920, a team made up of players from the St. Louis area accepted Sweden's invitation to tour, and they did well, too, going 7-2-5. Their smart, spirited play caused great excitement among the Swedish fans, and one newspaper predicted "It will not be a long time before American soccer football will surpass the playing of the Europeans."

During the 1920s the quality of soccer in America did indeed improve. The economy boomed, drawing millions of immigrants from the world's soccer-playing countries. At the same time, American workers were enjoying more leisure time than ever before. Semipro leagues flourished, with top players able to double the $30-a-week salaries they got from their regular jobs. Many factories formed teams, and in some cases their stars would be given no-show jobs to keep them from looking elsewhere for employment.

Bethlehem Steel continued to be a leader in the development of American soccer, thanks to Horace Lewis, a native Welshman who believed that the game could only become a major sport in the United States if fans believed that it was being played on a world-class level. In this regard, Lewis was a visionary. But the way he went about improving the American game left something to be desired. Rather than developing U.S. players, he and his brother, Wilbur, scouted the eastern seaboard's Irish, English, and Scottish communities and lured them to Bethlehem with cushy jobs. They even traveled to the British Isles in their search for talent. Other companies followed the lead of the Lewises, and by the mid-1920s it was hard to find more than one or two American-born players on the top American teams.

With so much talent available, a new pro circuit, the American Soccer League (ASL),

was formed, and it thrived during the 1920s, drawing as many as 20,000 fans a game. Many major-city newspapers had soccer editors, and the amateur game was thriving from high schools, to colleges, to club teams.

The first American-made soccer stars emerged during this period. One was named Archie Stark, and although he was born in Wales and spent his early childhood in Canada, he was a product of the soccer hotbed in Kearney, New Jersey. Stark made around $40 a week as a machinist in Manhattan and pocketed another $30 playing twice a week. He was roundly hailed as the finest player in the area, and when the Lewis brothers showed up to hire him for Bethlehem, he hammered out a deal that eventually made him the highest-paid soccer player in America. At the time, most connoisseurs of the sport considered Bethlehem's Wattie and Alex Jackson to be the two finest players in the country, but after one season, Stark had doubled their combined goal-scoring total.

The other notable native star was Davey Brown, an electrician by day and a deadly scorer on the weekends. He moved from team to team, making as much as $50 a game. He could do everything well—run, dribble, pass, tackle—and he once scored 53 goals in a season. He had a nose for the ball, especially in the penalty box, where he did the bulk of his scoring. There seems little doubt that he would have been an above-average player in any country during the 1920s, including England.

The United States fielded its first Olympic team in 1924. Although selected from the country's finest amateur players, it did not include any college stars. Its first game was a sloppy, rain-soaked affair against Estonia attended by 1,000 hissing French

This United States national team defeated a Canadian squad 6-1 on November 8, 1925.

fans, who were angry about a U.S. rugby victory over their national team the day before. Another game, played between Italy and Spain over in the Bergeyre Stadium at the same time, drew 30,000 spectators. The U.S. team's second game was played in the big stadium and drew a more respectable crowd, but it came against the dazzling Uruguayans, who won easily, 3-0. It was the first official soccer match between South American and North American teams, and it was most notable for a second-half adjustment made by the U.S team. Down three goals at the half, manager George Collins played just one fullback and four halfbacks in a highly unorthodox midfield "zone defense," totally baffling Uruguay for the final 45 minutes. It was a radical move, and as it turned out, the only defensive alignment that worked against Uruguay during the Olympics.

Soccer continued to thrive in the mid-1920s, and ASL teams became more and more aggressive about hiring foreign players, often without checking to see if their old teams had released them. The United States

Football Association (USFA) tried to stop this practice because it conflicted with FIFA regulations. The ASL responded by ordering its teams to boycott the USFA's Challenge Cup competition. Three teams refused, and withdrew from the ASL to start their own league, which was immediately sanctioned by the USFA. Then the USFA placed a blanket suspension on the ASL, which decided to ignore the USFA and operate as an "outlaw" league.

All the players wanted to do was play soccer and pocket their modest game fees. Most could not have cared less about who was bickering with whom. But when they realized that the ASL would operate in defiance of the USFA, dozens jumped ship in fear that they would receive lifetime suspensions from FIFA. To make matters even more complicated, the long-running Southern New York Football Association, which counted 170 clubs among its members, withdrew from the USFA, claiming it had violated its territorial rights by recognizing the new league.

The New York Nationals won the 1928 Challenge Cup championship, then fell prey to squabbles between the ASL and USFA.

Not until 1929 were all of these petty differences ironed out. By then, most of the foreign players who had won soccer so much popularity in the United States—including Alex Jackson, who would become a star in Scotland—got fed up and went back home. It was a crushing blow, and coupled with the Great Depression of the 1930s, it signaled the end of soccer's last best chance to become a major sport in the United States.

All of the infighting between various leagues and officials seriously undermined the formation of the 1928 U.S. Olympic team, which was blown out in Amsterdam. Luckily, all was calm when it came time to assemble a team for the first World Cup. The best player on the squad was center-half Billy Gonsalves, who had been a pro in Boston since the age of 17 and whose shot was so powerful and accurate he could score from 30 to 40 yards out. Gonsalves was the son of Portuguese immigrants, and he was the country's top player at the time. Twenty-one-year-old Bertram Patenaude was the

team's other young star. He scored five goals in Fall River's 1929 Challenge Cup victory over the Chicago Bricklayers club and, like Gonsalves, could have held his own in any league in the world.

Both men were instrumental in the team's opening-round victory against Belgium, and Patenaude went wild in the next match, scoring all the goals in a 3-0 shutout of Paraguay. Facing Argentina—the same team that had wiped them out in the 1928 Olympics—in the semifinals, the United States planned to mark their opponents closely. This strategy worked until a key player went down, and veteran goalie Jimmy Douglas twisted his knee. The floodgates opened, and the American net became a shooting gallery. The final score was 6-1.

The trip to Uruguay provided an interesting contrast in styles. The United States had big, athletic players who valued teamwork above all else. They made great use of their heads around the goal, making the most of the height advantage they possessed, and they employed long shots and passes

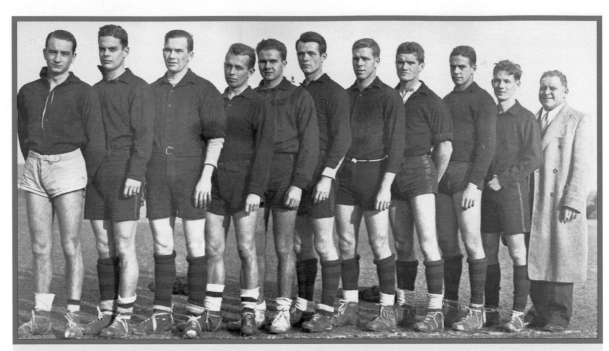

The 1932 Penn college team poses for a photograph.

thanks to their strong legs and comparatively burly frames. The South Americans, on the other hand, were quick, flashy stylists who valued finesse over raw power.

Professional soccer all but disappeared during the 1930s in the United States because of the Great Depression. The strong teams stayed afloat, but only drew big crowds for special exhibition games against touring clubs from other countries. Many of the teams sponsored by corporations disbanded, as those corporations teetered on the verge of bankruptcy. The ASL folded its tent for several years, leaving many top players with little choice but to play for a dollar or two a game. Soccer survived in the United States thanks in large part to strong semipro leagues run in the ethnic neighborhoods of the nation's largest cities. The USFA barely survived, run out of an office in a linen company by Joseph Barriskill.

Any hopes that the game might be revived at the 1932 Olympics in Los Angeles were dashed when the soccer competition was cancelled altogether. Most countries felt it was too expensive to send an entire team to the United States, and FIFA was reluctant to step in and help, fearing there might not be room enough for a World Cup and an Olympic tournament.

When World Cup '34 rolled around, the U.S. team was selected from players in a game between a top amateur team in Philadelphia and a collection of pros who were able to scrape together the train fare. Gonsalves was still the star, but a high-scoring amateur named Buff Donelli quickly asserted himself as a crucial member of the front line. The team crossed the Atlantic to Italy and got in a couple of practices before facing Mexico. Donelli scored four times in that game, showing exceptional speed in splitting defenders and great cunning in using opponents to screen his shots. Against Italy, however, Donelli's lone goal was all the scoring the Americans could muster, and they fell to the eventual champs, 7-1. After the final, Donelli was offered $5,000 to stay and play professionally in Italy, but he declined. Gonsalves also turned down several offers from European teams. Neither wanted to be in Europe with fascism on the rise and war seemingly on the horizon. Upon returning to the states, Gonsalves continued to make a living playing soccer, moving from team to team whenever a better pay day presented itself. He was perhaps the only soccer player in America who made a decent income during the 1930s—that is how bad things were in the sport. Donelli stopped playing soccer altogether and turned to football. Eventually, he became the coach of the NFL's Pittsburgh Steelers.

The United States was barely able to sponsor a team for the 1936 Olympics. A series of money-raising exhibition games in 1935 and 1936 was a disaster thanks to unexpectedly heavy snowfall, and Joe Barriskill had to come to the rescue with $6,700 in USFA funds in the eleventh hour so the team could go to Berlin. Unfortunately, America's first opponent was powerful Italy. To the surprise of 10,000 German spectators, the United States held its own in a hard, physical game and lost a 1-0 heartbreaker.

The United States failed to qualify for the World Cup in 1938, but the good news was that the ASL, restarted in 1935, was once again producing some pretty good soccer. Salaries were low and games poorly attended, but at least soccer was not completely dead. In 1939, Scotland sent its national team to the U.S. and drew a crowd of 25,000 at New York's Polo Grounds. The fans got their money's worth that day, as a

Billy Gonsalves was the best U.S. player in the early 1930s. He played on the U.S. national team in World Cup '30 and World Cup '34.

Official Rules of

FOOTBALL

AND SOCCER BALL

1938

Published by
WILSON SPORTING GOODS CO.

This 1938 rulebook contained the official rules for both football and soccer. The reference to the game as "soccer ball" illustrates how unfamiliar most Americans were with the game.

team of ASL all-stars battled the Scots to a thrilling 1-1 tie.

World War II

The years prior to World War II saw the emergence of more new stars in Europe, some of whom would come back after 1945 and some of whom would not. Among those who performed well pre- and post-war were Italy's Piola, who remained a top performer into the early 1950s, and a pair of Englishmen, Tommy Lawton and Stanley Matthews.

Lawton made headlines when he scored a hat trick at the age of 16, and he became one of England's top sharpshooters in the late 1930s. A great crowd favorite who continued to play top-notch soccer well into his thirties, Lawton was a genius at cashing in on transfer percentages by constantly switching clubs. Matthews played on the right wing, where he established himself as the best ever to play that position despite losing precious years to the war. Nicknamed the "Wizard of Dribble," he could beat any left halfback in the world one-on-one. Matthews would dribble right up to an opponent, feint one way and explode in the opposite direction. Everyone in the stadium knew what he was going to do when he got the ball, and yet—even in his forties—no one could stop him with any degree of consistency.

Between 1939 and 1945, the world sent its young men to war for the second time in 25 years. Soccer, however, did not die. Most countries offered their top players military posts as physical education instructors, and the game was played for recreation in training camps and behind the lines throughout the war. Most European leagues curtailed regular operation, as gatherings of large crowds were frowned upon during wartime. But many games were played to benefit relief charities and to boost morale for the men and women working to win the war on the home front. As the war dragged on and more and more prisoners were taken by each side, soccer actually flourished in many internment camps. British prisoners of war in Germany set up entire leagues in their camps, while German POWs did the same in England. One prisoner, Bert Trautmann, who had played halfback for Bremen in the German league, discovered he was a terrific goalie during his incarceration. When the

STANLEY MATTHEWS

Most fans are well aware of the awful toll that World War II took on professional sports in the United States. Some of the all-time greats in football, baseball, and hockey lost their prime years to the conflict, and many of America's budding young stars never got to fulfill their promise after returning from years of military service.

Imagine, then, the effect of the war on British soccer players. Their sport was all but abandoned. Their country was under attack through the air, and many of their finest players served in the military for up to seven years. Out of this mess emerged Stanley Matthews, an outrageously talented right wing who emerged from World War II with his skills undiminished.

Matthews was a top schoolboy soccer star and signed a pro contract in 1932 at the age of 17. At 18, he was a regular for the Stoke City club, and at 19 he made the English national team.

Playing on the right wing, Matthews terrorized defenders with one simple move. He would dribble slowly and deliberately toward an opponent until he was within a couple of yards, then shift his body quickly to the left or right. When the defender leaned one way, Matthews would dart the other way and move right past him.

Stanley Matthews is considered soccer's best player in first half of the 20th century.

Although it sounds simple, this move is extremely difficult. It requires world-class speed and flawless ballhandling, both of which Matthews possessed. Some say he was the quickest player ever over the first 10 yards.

"The Wizard of Dribble" became the most popular player in England while laboring for a mediocre Stoke City club. After the war, he transferred to Blackpool, where he led the club to the FA Cup final twice. Both times Matthews was on the losing side, however, and it seemed that time would run out on his brilliant career before he ever achieved the one prize that had eluded him.

But in 1953, Blackpool returned to the FA Cup and Matthews, 38, played the game of his life. With his team trailing 3-1 in the second half, Matthews took over, ripping Bolton's defense apart and lifting his team to a remarkable 4-3 win. During the match's waning minutes, he made several dramatic charges down the right side, leaving trails of hapless opponents sprawled out on the ground behind him. With 30 seconds left, he swerved past two Bolton players and booted a perfect cross to teammate Bill Perry, who scored the clincher as time ran out. To this day, the match is referred to as the Matthews Final.

In his 40s, Matthews still ranked among the top players in soccer. Indeed, he was selected as European Footballer of the Year in 1956 and 1963. He finally called it in 1965 and became the first soccer player to be knighted.

During World War II, German halfback Bert Trautmann (left) learned to play the goalkeeper position in an English prisoner-of-war camp. After the war, he stayed in England to play professionally. He won the Footballer of the Year award in 1956. Argentine Angel Labruna (right) was regarded as one of the best South American players during the 1940s.

war ended, he stayed in England and ended up playing for a club in St. Helens Town. In 1956, he led Manchester City to the FA Cup and was named English Footballer of the Year.

As had been the case during World War I, soccer was less affected in South America. During the 1940s, the River Plate club of Argentina flourished thanks to Adolfo Pedernera and Juan Moreno. These two—along with Miguel Muñoz, Angel Labruna, and Loustau—formed a front line so adept at scoring goals that it was called *La Maquina* (The Machine). Pedernera played center-forward throughout the late 1930s and 1940s, eventually giving way to a young man named Alfredo Di Stefano in 1946. Moreno joined River Plate in the mid-1930s as a teenager and by the 1940s had blos-

somed into one of the world's top inside-rights. In all, he played for teams in five different countries in a long and distinguished career that lasted into the 1950s.

The Postwar Years

In general, though, soccer was badly bruised and battered by World War II. Many of the world's familiar stars were either dead, retired, or had simply lost the best years of their careers. Most European countries lay in ruins, the people utterly exhausted from almost seven years of death and destruction. Enthusiasm for the game needed to be rekindled, and the spark would come from an improbable place.

In November 1945, just a few months after the war ended in Europe, a collection of unknown athletes from the Soviet Union embarked upon a tour of England. The team was called Moscow Dynamo, and they were welcomed with open arms by British fans. No one expected much of these players, so their warm reception had more to do with Russia's valiant effort as a British ally than anything else. Nearly 100,000 fans showed up for the first game against Chelsea, an incredible gate for a friendly exhibition contest. In the earliest recorded use of "Flower Power," the Russians won the hearts of the crowd—and probably psyched out their opponents—by presenting a bouquet of flowers to each Chelsea player before the contest began. As expected, Chelsea's pros netted two quick goals against the Russian amateurs. But then something magical happened. The sharp, creative passes of the visitors began to pay off, and they scored three of the match's final four goals to achieve a 3-3 tie. Dynamo left the field to a roaring ovation and suddenly everyone had to know everything there was to know about this wonderful group of young men.

The Dynamo players ate all their meals at the Soviet embassy. They insisted that one of their own referees work each game. And their acrobatic goalie was nicknamed "Tiger." But beyond that, they were an utter mystery. Interest in Dynamo continued to grow as they creamed Cardiff City 10-1 and then took on the Arsenal club, which added superstar Stanley Matthews to its lineup as a "special guest." A thick fog settled over the field, limiting visibility to about 25 feet. Normally, the game would have been cancelled, but Arsenal took a 3-1 lead and the decision was made to play on. Somehow in this eerie shroud—and with considerable help from their own referee—Dynamo scored three straight times to win, and their legend continued to grow. News started to spread throughout the soccer world of this great team, and the British players were starting to smart a little. In the tour's next game, against the Rangers, tempers began to flare as the Russians played to a 2-2 tie. Just prior to their next match, the Dynamo players boarded a plane and flew back to the Soviet Union without any explanation.

The Moscow Dynamo team walks onto the pitch at Stamford Bridge for their match against Chelsea on November 13, 1945.

The postwar years saw three interesting trends in soccer. First, as countries recovered from the devastation, attendance swelled at soccer matches all over the globe. Second, with the advances made in communications technology and the availability of paper after years of wartime shortages, soccer was receiving tremendous coverage on radio, in magazines and newspapers, and even on television. More fans in more countries knew more about the world soccer scene than ever before. And third, Moscow Dynamo was not the only "beasts from the east."

Indeed, several Eastern European countries that had come under the control of the Soviet Union after the war were busy forming tremendous soccer programs. With Communist governments in control, nations like Hungary, Bulgaria, and the Soviet Union could place their best players on one team, hire the best coaches, and construct world-class facilities. With these young athletes working, living, and playing together, the teams became tight, cohesive units. And because, under the Communist system, these teams were made up of "workers" rather than professional athletes, they were allowed to compete as amateurs in international competition. At the 1948 Olympics in London, gold medal winner Sweden became the last non-Communist country to win the Olympic soccer competition until the Soviet boycott in 1984. The runner-up in 1948 was Yugoslavia, which was on the verge of becoming a soccer power.

The Swedes won the gold medal in 1948 on the strength of the Nordhal brothers, a soccer-playing family led by Gunnar, a deadly finisher who cashed in on his Olympic fame and turned pro with AC Milan. Nordhal went on to lead the Italian league in scoring five times. Among the other top players to emerge right after the war was Scotland's George Young and Ireland's Johnny Carey. Young was an imposing defensive specialist who showed a delicate touch when he had to, especially on penalty kicks, which was something of a specialty for him. He played his entire career with the Rangers club, winning six Scottish league titles during that span. Carey also played his entire career with one team, Manchester United. He was adored by fans for his tremendous versatility and could play every position well—even, on occasion, goalkeeper. He captained United to the FA Cup in 1948 and later became a celebrated manager. Aside from this notable trio, there were not many new stars in European soccer until the early 1950s. The "pool" of young talent that would normally have produced soccer's young guns had been decimated by years of fighting.

This was not true in South America, of course. The sport had barely been affected during the war, meaning that the top players of the 1930s were available to impart their wisdom to the emerging players of the early 1940s, who in turn were around for the stars who burst upon the scene during the late 1940s. And there were plenty of them. In Brazil, center-forward Ademir de Menezes was flanked by insides Zizinho and Jair Da Rosa to form the heart of the national team. So adept a scorer was Ademir that opponents regularly added an extra central defender when they played his Vasco da Gama club. In Uruguay, the Peñarol team boasted a couple of top players in Obdulio Varela and Pepe Schiaffino. Varela developed nicely during the war years, ending the decade as one of the world's most offense-minded center-halfs. Schiaffino, an inside-forward, was Uruguay's biggest star in the late 1940s.

MONEY TALKS

In 1948, Argentine soccer players staged a strike against their clubs, demanding higher pay. At the same time, a group of investors in Colombia was attempting to start a professional league in that country. The only problem is that they were unwilling to cough up the large transfer fees required to bring international stars to their country. They decided to bypass the normal transfer procedure and sign players directly.

Their first move was to sign the great center-forward Adolfo Pedernera to the Bogotá club, giving them a big name to help lure other top players. One by one, the Colombian league signed away Argentina's top players, including halfback Nestor Rossi and goalie Julio Cozzi. The big prize was Alfredo Di Stefano, who was on the verge of becoming the best player in the world. The most successful team was Pedernera's Millonarios, or millionaires, so named because of the huge salaries paid to its best players.

Of course, this method of signing star players was a gross violation of FIFA rules, thus the Colombian league was considered a "pirate" league. Despite FIFA's threat to severely punish any player who signed on, dozens from around the world took the money and joined the league. Eventually, poor attendance drove the Colombian league out of business, but not before the Millonarios club—nicknamed the "Blue Ballet" for its fine play and striking uniforms—made a lucrative farewell tour, playing before packed stadiums all over the world.

FIFA reconvened right after the war and decided to resume the World Cup. It voted to hold the first two tournaments in countries that had not been ravaged by war, so Brazil was awarded the 1949 tournament, and Switzerland would play host in 1953. The dates were changed to 1950 and 1954 when it became evident that more time would be needed to prepare for the huge crowds expected to attend.

World Cup '50

As anticipated, World Cup '50 was met with great enthusiasm. The Brazilians had an awesome team, and the English would be sending a contingent to the World Cup for the first time. Clearly, the final would be a showdown between these two soccer powers. But in what may have been the wildest World Cup ever, neither of these giants prevailed. The English went out early, losing to—of all teams—a rag-tag contingent from the United States. This group included college players, amateurs, and several stars from Sunday professional leagues. The top scorer for the United States was Joe Gaetjens, a Haitian-American who had been washing dishes at a Brooklyn restaurant where a local soccer team ate its pregame

FIFA president Jules Rimet shakes hands with Argentina's goalie Miguel Rugilo at Wembley Stadium on May 11, 1951. Rimet was the guiding force behind FIFA.

meals. He asked for a tryout and became the starting center-forward that very day! Gaetjens scored the only goal in the win over England with a header late in the first half. Disheartened and embarrassed, England went out meekly with a 1-0 loss to Spain. At home, the London papers pronounced British soccer dead.

As expected, Brazil made it all the way to the final. There it met a Uruguayan squad that had qualified for the tournament when Peru and Ecuador pulled out. Because of a complicated new round-robin format, Brazil could have won the World Cup even with a tie, so it was with tremendous anticipation that 199,854 fans jammed into Maracana Stadium to root for the local boys. The oddsmakers made Brazil a 10-1 favorite, and each player would take home the then-princely sum of $20,000 once they were

crowned World Cup champions. But the game did not go as planned. After a scoreless first half, Brazil broke the deadlock, but Uruguay's Varela came right back and knotted the score at 1-1 after some critical miscommunication between Brazil's coach and his players. Then, instead of playing for the tie, Brazil placed the Uruguayan goal under siege for the rest of the match. Not only did the visitors survive, they actually managed to counterattack, and Pepe Schiaffino scored before a dead-silent stadium to give Uruguay an improbable 2-1 win. Even in retrospect, the victories by Uruguay and the United States defy explanation. If those games were replayed 100 times, it seems doubtful that either team would win again.

The Magic Magyars

Students of postwar soccer are quick to point out that, had Hungary been able to send a team to the World Cup in 1950, these dramatics might never have occurred. From 1943 to 1956, the national team—nicknamed The Magic Magyars—did not lose a game on its home soil, and from 1950 to 1954 they played 29 straight games, at home and away, without a single defeat. The team befuddled opponents by taking the emphasis off the center-forward and working the ball in from the sides. Hungary's center played back, almost at midfield, while the insides and the wings pressed the attack. Meanwhile, four defenders played back to guard the goal.

At the 1952 Olympics in Helsinki, Finland, Hungary rolled over its opponents. In five games, the Magyars scored 20 goals and allowed just two. In goalie Gyula Grosics, halfback Jozsef Bozsik and forwards Sandor Kocsis and Nandor Hidegkuti, Hungary could boast four of the finest players in the world. And in 25-year-old captain Ferenc Puskas, the team had the man some consider soccer's most dynamic player of the 1950s.

Puskas, at inside-left, and Kocsis, at inside-right, spearheaded Hungary's unstoppable offense. Center-forward Hidegkuti would lay back, creating all sorts of problems for opposing fullbacks, who were hesitant to leave their posts and guard him closely. To make matters worse, the three could practically read each other's thoughts, and often worked as one, changing positions on the fly without breaking the flow of the attack. Behind them was Bozsik, setting up plays from his position at right halfback and often pressing the attack himself. It was a brand new approach that created plenty of scoring opportunities for all four players, but

Football

Ferenc Puskas

Hungarian forward Ferenc Puskas was one of the world's best players in the 1950s.

in fairness to Hungary's often-overwhelmed opponents, it only worked because of the immense talent involved.

That talent proved too much for England, which lost 6-3 to Hungary in a 1952 match at London's Wembley Stadium. It was England's first home loss in international play, and it was a decisive one. Hidegkuti drilled three goals, Puskas two, and Bozsik chipped one in from outside to cap the scoring. In a return meeting played in Budapest, Hungary, they annihilated the English 7-1. By the time World Cup '54 rolled around, everyone was handing the Jules Rimet Trophy to the Magyars. Despite a very strong field, it appeared no one had the talent to touch Hungary, which had not lost a game in more than four years.

World Cup '54

West German coach Sepp Herberger was among those who knew it would take something extraordinary to beat the Hungarians. But in the new pool format—where the top two teams in each grouping would advance to the quarterfinal round—he saw his chance. West Germany, Hungary, and weak teams from Turkey and South Korea were all in Pool 2. Herberger calculated that by pulling his best players and losing to Hungary, his team would sidestep the Brazilians in the next round and enter the semifinal game in far better condition than any opponent it might face. Brazil was a dangerous team. Though not favored to win the Cup, they were still smarting from the loss to Uruguay in the 1950 final. Their star, an inside-forward named Didi, was a master setup man and a magician when it came to free kicks.

Playing only five regulars against Hun-

The Hungarian team, pictured here prior to the final World Cup '54, were a powerhouse during the 1950s.

gary, West Germany lost 8-3, as Kocsis scored four times. The strategy worked better than Herberger had hoped, for not only did his team end up playing Yugoslavia instead of Brazil in the next round, but Puskas had sustained a severe injury in the game and would not be playing at full speed for the remainder of the tournament. So it was that Hungary had the unenviable task of playing the Brazilians in the quarterfinals. Desperate to gain an advantage, Brazil came out and played a dirty, physical game. The Hungarians responded in kind, and the match quickly deteriorated into an endless stream of infractions and fistfights. At one point, Bozsik and Brazil's Nilton Santos had to be escorted off the field by local police. After the game, which Hungary won 4-2, there was another melee between the players in the stadium tunnel.

Meanwhile, the West Germans had an easy time with Yugoslavia and advanced to the final with a convincing win over Austria. There they met the exhausted Magyars, who had disposed of pesky Uruguay 4-2 but had required extra time to do so. Puskas was still hurt but insisted on playing, and he scored one of Hungary's two goals in the first eight minutes. West Germany came right back to knot the score at 2-2. The game settled into a grim, defensive battle, which was decided on a mistake. A poor clearance by a Hungarian defender was picked up by Helmut Rahn, and he fired it past Groscis for his second goal of the game. Puskas, spectacular to the very end, drilled what appeared to be the equalizer with two minutes left, but offside was called and the goal waved off. It took a combination of strategy, luck, and clutch play, but the Magic Magyars were finally defeated.

A New Cup

By the mid-1950s, soccer was thriving in nearly every country in the world. Professional leagues were drawing millions of fans in Great Britain, France, Spain, Italy, Germany, and in such Latin American countries as Brazil, Mexico, Uruguay, and Argentina.

West Germany scores a goal in the 1954 World Cup final. The upset favored Hungarian team 3–2.

Although rules existed limiting the number of "foreign" players in these leagues, the sport's top stars moved freely from team to team. Soccer had become truly international, as fans in one country typically tracked the progress of important players and teams in other countries. How would the best team in, say, the Spanish League do against the best from, say, Italy? In the years following the war, this kind of question was decided by scheduling special exhibition games, which were immensely popular and well-attended.

After the 1954 Olympics, the Wolverhampton Wanderers played Hungary's Honved club in just such a match and scored three goals in the final three minutes to stun Puskas and company 3-2. Chelsea fans quickly proclaimed their Wolves the official champions of Europe. This irritated the rest of the soccer world and underscored the need for an annual club championship, which would bring together the best pro teams.

In 1956, the European Cup was established by the European Union of Football As-

sociations, creating a tournament that brought together the regular-season champions of all the major leagues. Sixteen professional clubs were invited to participate, and Real Madrid of Spain beat French champion Reims 4-3 in the final, which was held in Paris. During this inaugural competition, the soccer world discovered the considerable talents of Alfredo Di Stefano, the Argentine-born center-forward who led Real Madrid to a comeback win in the final. Di Stefano was a deadly scorer, but he was hardly a one-way player. When the other team attacked, he would take an active role in the defense, standing guard at the top of the penalty area and initiating counterattacks with dramatic charges through Madrid's retreating opponents.

The first European Cup also marked the end of Hungarian dominance. While its entry in the tournament was playing Italian power Bilbao, Hungary erupted in revolution. Soviet tanks rolled into Budapest and crushed the rebellion, tightening the U.S.S.R.'s grip on the Hungarian people. Puskas, who had scored 83 goals in 84 inter-

ALFREDO DI STEFANO

On the soccer field, Alfredo Di Stefano always seemed to be in the right place at the right time.

For the first century of soccer, the idea of an "all-around" player was limited to proficiency in the basic skills of the game, such as dribbling and shooting. In the 1950s, Alfredo Di Stefano made fans understand that there was another level a player could reach.

Di Stefano and his brother, Tulio, learned soccer in the tough street games played in Buenos Aires, Argentina, and he built up his legendary stamina working on the family's farm outside the city. By their late teens, the brothers were playing for the local club, albeit against the wishes of their father, who felt that soccer was a frivolous way to earn a living.

Alfredo Di Stefano made the River Plate team at 17 as a right wing, but his dream was to become a center-forward like his hero, Arsenio Erico, who starred for Independiente during the late 1930s. But with all-time great Adolfo Pedernera playing the position for River Plate, there seemed little chance that he would fill that slot. In a stroke of good luck, Di Stefano was loaned to the Huracan club for a couple of seasons, where he blossomed at the center position. So good had he become that River Plate sent Pedernera to another club and installed Di Stefano in the heart of its awesome, five-man front line that was known the world over as *La Maquina* (The Machine).

River Plate won the South American championship in 1947, and young Di Stefano was soaking up the wisdom of his veteran teammates and incorporating it into his game, which seemed to get better every day. A players' strike in 1948 prompted him to jump to the Millonarios club of the pirate Colombian league, where he became the circuit's top player. Before the league folded, Millonarios embarked on a world exhibition tour, and Di Stefano established himself as the finest player on the field, even against the top stars in Europe. He was particularly brilliant during Real Madrid's 50th anniversary soccer tournament, and the club signed him to a contract on the spot.

He was peerless in nearly every aspect of the game, but beyond that, he seemed able to marshal his teammates around him in such a way as to maximize his own skills as well as their own. Within a year of Di Stefano's arrival, Real Madrid became the best club in Europe. When the European Cup was established in 1956, Real Madrid won it five times in a row. In the 1960 final against Frankfurt, Di Stefano netted a hat trick in a 7-3 rout that ranks among the great matches in history.

Throughout his career, which concluded after the 1964–65 season, Di Stefano specialized in being in the right place at the right time, whether it was thwarting a shot in his own penalty area, initiating an attack at midfield, or crashing the ball into the net at the other end.

national contests, decided not to return to his country. His defection ripped the heart out of the Hungarian team.

Hungary's loss was Spain's gain. In 1958, Puskas—whom some considered over-the-hill at 31—signed with the Real Madrid club and proceeded to lead the Spanish league in scoring four times. He and Di Stefano packed a one-two punch that ranks among the greatest of all time, and together they won the European Cup five straight years. Their greatest moment came in the 1960 final against Eintracht Frankfurt, when Di Stefano hit for three goals and Puskas got four in a 7-3 victory. Supporting these two superstars was Luis Del Sol, a hardworking midfielder who later starred for Juventus of the Italian league. Another key player for Real Madrid was Francisco Gento, who would launch shots from the left wing with such force that fans called him "El Supersonico." Gento went on to win 12 league titles and a record six European Cups.

As Hungary's star fell during the final years of the 1950s, other teams from the Eastern Bloc rose to replace them. The Soviet Union dominated at the 1956 Olympics in Melbourne, Australia, behind the spectacular work of goalie Lev Yashin. Nicknamed "The Black Octopus," Yashin was Russia's first international superstar. He had a knack for outguessing shooters, which enabled him to stop shots no one else could even touch. Indeed, over his long career, he stopped more than 150 penalty kicks! Also on the Soviet squad were world-class stars Igor Netto, Valentin Ivanov, and Nikita Simonyan. In 1960, this group prevailed in the first European Championship, an event for national teams held between the World Cups.

Also on the rise was Yugoslavia, which in Australia had been an Olympic silver medal-

ist for the third consecutive time. The problem was not a lack of talent but perhaps too much talent. Under the regime of Marshall Tito, which was far less restrictive than that of other Communist countries, Yugoslavian players were free to cross the border and play professionally for other European clubs. So many fine players were scattered across so many good teams, that it was almost impossible to pull together a national squad in time to practice and play together prior to international competition. Finally, Yugoslavia struck gold in the 1960 Olympics, beating Denmark 3-1 in the final. Ironically, luck played as much a part in this victory as talent. After tying Bulgaria in the preliminary round, the

Soccer

Lev Yashin

Soviet goalkeeper Lev Yashin (right), pictured here in a Dynamo Moscow uniform, was known as the Black Octopus because of his amazing ability to stop shots.

team advanced by winning a coin toss. In the final, captain Milan Galic opened the game with an impossible goal from 30 yards out. He was ejected for insulting a referee 40 minutes later, leaving his teammates to hang on with just 10 players.

Finally, during this decade, the game in England continued to be excellent, despite the "death of football" trumpeted by British newspaper headlines in 1950. Among the world-class players produced in the British Isles were John Charles, perhaps the finest player ever to come out of Wales. Charles was dubbed "The Gentle Giant," and he was brilliant at center-half or center-forward. Eventually, he took his talents to Juventus of the Italian league, where he became one of Italy's most popular stars. Most notable among those who stayed was winger Tom Finney, a complete all-around performer who played his entire career with the mediocre Preston club.

Europe on the Rise

By the late 1950s, European soccer was at full strength once again. World-class players were coming out of every country, and for the first time there was a measure of parity between the various national leagues. In France, Raymond Kopa was one of many fine players on a Reims club that still ranks among the best in history. Originally a right wing, Kopa moved inside where he could make better use of his creativity, and his career took off. After a brief stint with Real Madrid, he returned to Reims and was named European Footballer of the Year, a prestigious award instituted in 1956. Kopa's teammates included center René Bliard, and a strong left side anchored by Jean Vincent and Roger Piatoni. Vying for playing time

on what was to be one of the last great five-man forward lines was a young center-forward named Just Fontaine.

Neighboring Belgium could boast one of the game's top scorers—and one of its first "bad boys"—in Rik Coppens. He was a relentless, aggressive attacker who sometimes had trouble hitting the off switch when he left the field, tangling regularly with teammates, fans, and even club officials. In Central and Eastern Europe, soccer got a big boost from the emergence of Gerhard Hanappi and Ivan Kolev. Hanappi spent his best years with the Rapid club of Vienna, where he won five Austrian championships. One of the most versatile performers in history, Hanappi put in quality time at nearly every position. Off the field, he proved equally versatile, earning an architectural degree and designing a new stadium for Rapid that was eventually named after him. Kolev was the best player Bulgaria had ever produced, and he drew favorable comparisons to the Hungarian Puskas. He spent his entire career with the Bulgarian army club, where he dominated the left side of their offense and led the team to 11 national championships.

England continued to develop world-class footballers during this period, most notably Ivor Allchurch, one of the classiest forwards in soccer. Allchurch did not have the look of a prolific scorer, but he had a real knack for putting the ball in the net. Sadly, his best years were wasted on mediocre clubs. The top team of the 1950s in England was the Wolverhampton Wanderers, or Wolves, who were led by halfback Billy Wright and wings Johnny Hancocks and Jimmy Mullen, who specialized in booting the long passes that keyed the team's high-scoring offense.

The best of the young English footballers might have been young Duncan Edwards, who like Di Stefano, always seemed to be at the center of things regardless of where the ball was being played. Edwards belonged to Manchester United, which won the first division title in 1956 and 1957. He was one of the "Busby Babes," a group of young players recruited and coached by manager Matt Busby, who created a sort of farm system to feed talent into United's starting lineup as its first-stringers got old or injured. In 1956, the average age of the team was just 23, and after winning the division, Busby defied the Football League's orders and took his boys to compete in the 1957 European Cup. He did the same in 1958, with tragic results. The team's plane crashed in a snowstorm at the Munich Airport and eight players, including the 21-year-old Edwards, were killed.

World Cup '58

The soccer world's spirits brightened a few months after the Munich tragedy as World Cup '58 opened in Stockholm, Sweden. In the years since the war, it had become the global event Jules Rimet had envisioned, and although he passed away in 1956, he could already see how big the 1958 competition would be. More than 50 countries competed for 16 spots in the tournament, and 1,500 journalists from around the world applied for press credentials. For the first time, the games would be televised to an international audience, with an anticipated viewership of 40 million, and 56 countries sent radio crews to cover the event.

There was much excitement over the entrants, too. Italy and Uruguay had failed to qualify, opening the door for some new faces. The Soviet team came with its great goalie Yashin. England was minus four starters because of the Manchester United crash but had emotion on its side. France had a meteoric young wing in Fontaine, and West Germany was still dangerous. Meanwhile, Argentina came in as South American champion.

Then there was Brazil, which fielded the most intriguing team in the tournament. Manager Vincente Feola employed his version of the 4-2-4 formation that had worked so well for Hungary—a system that put enough men back to stop opponents, while at the same time enabling the team to counterattack quickly without exposing the goal. If the cup were awarded to the team with the most character, charisma, eccentricity, and pure skill, then Brazil would have been the

Matt Busby is pictured here near the end of his playing career. Busby went on to coach legendary teams for Manchester United.

hands-down winner. But time after time, in international competition, the team would find a way to come undone. This time, however, Brazil had a plan, a team psychiatrist and a little surprise named Pelé.

Edson Arantes do Nascimento had been called Pelé as long as he could remember. At the age of 15, he earned a spot on the powerful Santos club when he walked into a practice and dribbled the length of the field, eluding 10 of Brazil's best professionals. The Santos coach signed him right away, after being assured that his players had not concocted an elaborate practical joke. Pelé scored a goal in his first start for Santos and

easily made the national team two years later. Still, when the Brazilians arrived in Sweden, the names most familiar to soccer fans were those of his teammates: Didi, Garrincha, Nilton Santos, and captain Luz Bellini. In fact, Pelé did not even play in the team's first two games because of a sore knee, and the papers did not even remark on his absence.

In those games, Brazil beat Austria but could manage only a scoreless tie with England. In the team meeting that followed, the leading players asked Feola to insert their young star, and he obliged. What followed began the transformation of a sport. Pelé en-

Brazil's World Cup '58 team poses with the Jules Rimet trophy. The 1958 World Cup competition launched the international career of a young superstar named Pelé.

ergized his team in a defeat of the Soviet Union, causing its coach Gabriel Katchalin to exclaim, "I can't believe that what we saw this afternoon was soccer. I have never seen anything so beautiful in my life."

In the quarterfinals, Pelé saved his team against an imposing eleven from Wales with his first World Cup goal. In the semis, he outscored French sharpshooter Fontaine—who netted a record 13 goals during the tournament—with a hat trick in a 5-2 win that got Brazil to the final against Sweden. There Pelé placed his indelible stamp upon soccer, as he quite literally took the world's breath away. With Brazil up 2-1, Pelé received a high pass with his back to the goal. He deadened the ball with his thigh, let it drop to the crook of his ankle, popped it up in the air, then did a back flip and rifled the ball past the awestruck Swedish goalkeeper. Brazil won the game easily, and had its first World Cup. And the legend of Pelé had become an international story.

The Brazilian victory is seen as the turning of a page in soccer's history. It marked the first time a World Cup had been won by a team playing outside its hemisphere. It also heralded the arrival of a player who clearly was on a higher level than everyone else. Yet what is most important—and most overlooked about Brazil's victory—is that, as a team, the players accomplished something that the soccer world had been progressing toward for a dozen years. The Brazilians played the same smart, trapping defense pioneered by teams such as Uruguay, but they added to it the crisp passing, fluid movement and opportunistic scoring of the great Hungarian teams. And they did so with the kind of style, drama, and flair that really turned people on. In the end, World Cup '58 provided new, spectacular models for the game's players, its teams, and its tournaments. Soccer was ready to move into the future.

U.S. Decline

While soccer was making great strides throughout the world, it was dying in the United States. The decade had looked so promising following the 1950 World Cup victory over England. There was great interest in the U.S. team, especially on the part of fans outside the United States. They wanted to see this wonder team that had beaten the British stars, and the people who ran the game at the international level wanted very much to bring the United States into the fold. They knew that if soccer in the States were to develop even to the point of, say, pro basketball or hockey—which were not yet major sports in the early 1950s—it would create a powerful new market for the game.

But once again, politics prevented U.S. soccer from growing. The USSFA refused most of the invitations to play abroad and totally failed to promote the sport at home. The association did propose a home-and-away "rematch" between England and the United States, which was met with a predictable refusal. English soccer was fast losing its dominance; it did not need the upstart Americans around to remind them of this. So in the end, not much came of the World Cup win. Three players, including Gaetjens, parlayed their talents into pro contracts abroad. The U.S. team did manage to play several overseas exhibitions, including a match against Scotland that drew more than 107,000 spectators. Clearly, soccer was interested in America, but there was little interest on the part of America in soccer.

Pelé, pictured here in 1962, led his Santos club to World Club Cup championships in 1962 and 1963. He played soccer professionally for 22 years and was considered the greatest player in the world.

PELÉ

In the history of sports, there have been a handful of special athletes who transcended their game, their time, and especially the skills of everyone playing around them. In basketball, that player would be Michael Jordan. In baseball, it was Babe Ruth. Football had Jim Brown; hockey had Wayne Gretzky; boxing had Muhammad Ali; and track and field had Carl Lewis. In soccer, that player was Pelé. He burst upon the scene at World Cup '58 at the age of 17, leading Brazil to victory and playing the game on such an astounding level that he was immediately hailed as the best footballer in history.

Born in the desperately poor village of Tres Coracoes, Edson Arantes do Nascimento did nothing but work on his soccer skills from the time he could walk. Wherever he went, he would kick something in front of him—a wadded-up sock, bundle of rags, rotten grapefruit, tin can, or crumpled newspaper—and at sometime early in his life, people began calling him Pelé, which is believed to be a play on the word *pelota*, or ball. Pelé's father was a semipro player who earned a few dollars a game to support the family, but when he injured his knee and had to quit the sport, responsibility for generating that extra income fell to his young son. By the age of 12, Pelé was the best player in the region, and at 15 he had earned a spot on Brazil's powerful Santos club.

In his first full season with Santos, Pelé scored a record 65 goals. And after his coming-out party in Stockholm at World Cup '58, he renegotiated his contract and became the highest-paid team sports athlete in the world. Santos was happy to pay him, for they knew in Pelé they had soccer's first international drawing card. Right after the World Cup, club officials began setting up a world tour to showcase their young star, sometimes playing three games a week. The millions they raked in enabled Santos to purchase the best players in Brazil as Pelé's supporting cast, and this group formed the nucleus of the team that won the World Club Cup in 1962 and 1963.

Still just a teenager, he went on to score a mind-boggling 127 goals in 1959. Between the years 1958 and 1973, Pele led Santos to 11 Brazilian championships and scored more than 1,200 league goals, and he also netted close to 100 goals in 108 international matches. He won every award imaginable, from South American Player of the Year to North American Soccer League (NASL) MVP. In World Cup competition, Brazil lost just once when he was in the lineup and was a perfect 8-0 when he scored a goal. Pelé scored 12 World Cup goals in 14 matches, and he is still the only man to play for three World Cup champions.

In 1969, Pelé scored his 1,000th Brazilian league goal in his 909th match before 80,000 fans and a national television audience. Two years later he played his final game for the national team, this time with 180,000 fans in attendance, all of whom chanted *Fica! Fica!* (Stay! Stay!) throughout the match. He retired from the Santos team in 1974 but soon took his skills to the United States, the only place in the world where he was not instantly recognized. Some wondered why, after dominating the top levels of soccer for 15 years, Pelé would want to play in a place where people did not appreciate what he had accomplished and did not understand the game he so loved. But those people missed the point.

"I looked and saw another mountain to climb," he explained. He worked his magic on the field and off, appearing on talk shows, conducting clinics, and making public appearances everywhere his team, the New York Cosmos, played. He drew huge crowds to every game, and he blazed a path for the international stars who soon followed him to the North American Soccer League. Pelé was crowned league MVP in 1976, then led the Cosmos on a highly successful world tour. In 1977, the team won the NASL championship. Pelé put professional soccer on the map during his time in the United States, instantly boosting annual NASL attendance from a few hundred thousand into the millions. His final match, a game between the Cosmos and the Brazilian national team, still ranks among the most moving in the history of sports. He played for New York in the first half, then switched uniforms to play for his country in the second half. The event drew 75,000 people and was broadcast to 38 countries around the world. As always, Pelé did not disappoint, scoring for both sides.

Pelé planted the seeds of soccer in the United States. When he arrived in 1974, barely 100,000 players were registered with the U.S. Soccer Federation. By the time he left, there were nearly half a million. Today, that figure stands at around two million; there are also 13 million kids under the age of 18 playing the sport and more college soccer teams than football teams. In 1983, Pelé began a personal lobbying campaign to bring the World Cup to the United States. In 1988, FIFA announced that America would host World Cup '94, proving Pelé had as much clout off the field as on, and securing his legacy in the United States for all time.

The situation worsened as the years rolled on. At the 1952 Olympics, the Americans failed to score a single goal. In 1953, a highly anticipated match between England and the United States at Yankee Stadium was postponed just two hours before game time because of a light drizzle, even as a baseball double header was played as scheduled across the river in the Polo Grounds. When the teams met the next night, fewer than 8,000 people showed up to watch. A few months later, the team failed to qualify for a World Cup berth. In 1956, the U.S. team was blown out by Yugoslavia in the first round of the Olympics. And in 1957, the team again failed to earn a World Cup bid for 1958. The English team returned to the United States for a match in 1959 and humiliated the U.S. squad 8-1 in Los Angeles. Again, attendance was sparse, and spectators had to be reminded that they could not keep the ball when it was kicked into the stands. British reporters traveling with the team ridiculed the American fans and wrote off U.S. players as third-rate. The lone bright spot for American soccer during the late 1950s came in 1959, when the national team placed third in the Pan Am Games with impressive wins over Mexico and Brazil.

On the field, there seemed to be little hope for soccer in America. But off the field, pro sports in the United States were on the verge of a major boom. Plans for professional leagues abounded, with television revenue and exposure the brass ring everyone was grasping for. Despite a lack of talent and little interest among mainstream sports fans, with so much money and enthusiasm being generated, surely even soccer would find a way to go "big time."

Cup Crazy

From Brazil's stunning success in 1958 there came great demand in the soccer world for a competition that would create a showdown between the best South American players and the top performers in Europe. This demand was met with the creation of the World Club Cup in 1960. It would pit the top European club, as decided by the European Cup, against South America's best professional team. The South American entrants were determined by the winner of the Copa Libertadores, which determined the top club on the continent starting in 1960.

The Peñarol (Uruguay), Santos (Brazil) and Independiente (Argentina) clubs dominated in the early part of the decade, while the Estudiantes de la Plata (Argentina) and Nacional (Uruguay) clubs came on strong in the late 1960s. This championship brought the soccer world closer together and created year-long interest among fans on both sides of the Atlantic.

It also created an international stage *without* the national fervor of the World Cup for the game's greatest stars. The first World Club Cup featured Real Madrid—with the high-scoring duo of Puskas and Di Stefano—against Uruguay's Peñarol club. Originally, it was a best-of-three format, with one game played in each home stadium and a tie-breaking match played immediately after, if necessary. The two teams played to a scoreless tie in the Uruguayan capital of Montevideo then met again in Spain two months later, where Madrid won easily, 5-1. Eventually, the World Club Cup became a one-game showdown. During the 1960s, this competition showcased the talents of Brazilian stars Garrincha and Pelé;

Sandro Mazzola of Italy; England's George Best and Bobby Charlton; Alberto Spencer, William Martinez, and Nestor Goncalves of Uruguay; Scotland's Tommy Gemmell; and Eusebio, the African-born superstar of Portuguese soccer.

The 1960s also saw the introduction of the European Cup-Winners' Cup. As in American sports, the team with the best regular-season record does not always win in the post-season, so whereas the European Cup was a competition of first-place finishers in various leagues, the field for the Cup-Winners' Cup was comprised of the season-ending playoff winners in the various national leagues. It did not always work out as planned—some countries did not have playoff tournaments, and sometimes the same team that finished first won the whole thing—but the soccer world had gone completely "cup-crazy" at this point, so the Cup-Winners' Cup was an immediate hit.

The UEFA Cup, which began in the late 1950s, also came of age during this period. Designed as a competition between the best players in Europe's major cities, it was called the Fairs Cup for the first several years of its existence. Competing cities were invited to field all-star squads from their top professional clubs, but some chose to have one club—with a guest player or two—as its representative. [It was the equivalent, perhaps, of an NHL game between the best players from California (Sharks, Kings, and Mighty Ducks) against the top players in the New York metropolitan area (Rangers, Devils, and Islanders).] This competition also gave Europe's top stars a chance to shine on the international stage, even if the clubs they played on were not successful. These games were typically tight, closely played affairs in front of packed stadiums. Other Cup competitions started in the 1960s included the African Champions Cup and the CONCACAF Champions Cup, held between Central American and Caribbean countries.

World Cup '62

The biggest Cup of all, of course, was still the World Cup, and fans spent the four years between 1958 and 1962 feverishly debating the merits of the Brazilian team. Could they possibly do it again? Could they possibly be beaten? The team's performance—and Pelé's in particular—had been so breathtaking that people were going crazy in anticipation. That Santos would represent South America in the 1962 World Club Cup meant soccer fans would be treated to a double dose of Pelé that year.

As it turned out, the Brazilians were so good they did not even need Pelé. That was fortunate, because they lost him to a pulled thigh muscle in their second World Cup match. In his place played a young unknown named Amarildo. (Like most Brazilian players, his given name was so long that he simply went by his first name.) Brazil trailed Spain 1-0 when Amarildo took control of the match and scored the clincher in a 2-1 win. From there, the great Garrincha came on, scoring twice to bury host country Chile in the first half of their semifinal and send Brazil to the final. There they encountered Czechoslovakia, the same team against whom Pelé had suffered his early-round injury. That first meeting ended in a scoreless tie, but this was not the case in the final, as the Czechs banged home an early goal for a 1-0 lead. Brazil kept cool and knotted the score two minutes later on a difficult angle shot by Amarildo. In the second half, Pelé's replacement put a perfect cross in front of

Soccer

Garrincha

Garrincha was voted most outstanding player of the 1962 World Cup for leading Brazil to the championship. Born Manoel Francisco dos Santos, he received his nickname for his love of chasing *garrinchas,* or Brazilian sparrows, as a child.

the goal and watched as teammate Zito headed it in. Vava then scored on a fumbled ball by Czech goalie Viliam Schroif to make the final tally 3-1.

Pelé did give the fans a thrill in the World Club Cup, scoring five goals in two games versus Portugal's Benfica club to give Santos the World Club championship. And he returned to the world stage again the following year, leading Santos to another club championship against Milan.

Besides Pelé's Santos bunch, the leading clubs of the early 1960s were Peñarol and Benefica. Long the top team in Uruguay,

Peñarol won the Copa Libertades in 1960 and 1961 and the World Club Cup in 1961. They were led by a trio of talented stars, including William Martinez and Nestor Goncalves. Their best player, however, was Alberto Spencer, who began his career in his native Ecuador. One of the world's best strikers, Spencer was an immensely popular and intelligent player who was accorded a unique honor for an athlete when he was named Ecuador's diplomatic consul in Uruguay.

Benfica, which played in the Portuguese capitol of Lisbon, reached the European Cup final four times, winning it all in 1961 and 1962. The team was captained by center-forward José Aguas, and the fireworks were supplied by Joaquim Santana and by Eusebio, who ranks among the best players in history. Many of Benfica's key players, including Eusebio, were born in the Portuguese colonies of Mozambique and Angola, where the country's richest clubs financed junior soccer programs to discover and then develop players.

The team that spoiled Benfica's bid for a third European Cup was Manchester United, which had bounced back from the 1958 Munich air disaster and restocked itself with some fine players. Chief among them was Bobby Charlton, one of the survivors of that terrible crash. Charlton possessed a booming shot and a knack for scoring dramatic goals. But it was young George Best who did in Benfica in the 1966 quarterfinals. Ignoring Matt Busby's instructions to lay back and contain the explosive Portuguese scorers, Best went crazy and netted a pair of goals early in the match. His teammates then followed his lead and scored a remarkable 5-1 victory. Best, whose dashing good looks reminded everyone of the Beatles, became an international heartthrob. He also developed into one of soccer's most talented and temperamental superstars.

The veteran Charlton was to be the focal point of England's soccer renaissance. As host of World Cup '66, England could ill afford to produce yet another poor showing. Right after World Cup '62, plans were laid to produce a true world-class team within four years. The first move was to hire a full-time manager for the national squad. That man was Alf Ramsey, a popular hero from the 1950s and someone with the reputation and expertise to select and train the players of his own choosing. Although the team stumbled in its first few international matches, by the summer of 1963, they had knocked off Czechoslovakia, East Germany, and Switzerland in away games. The normally reserved Ramsey saw something special in his men and boldly predicted they would win the World Cup in 1966.

MANCHESTER U.

O. RIGHT
GEORGE BEST

George Best was voted Footballer of the Year for 1967–68. Spanish-speaking fans called him El Beatle because he looked like a member of The Beatles, a British pop group.

World Cup '66

By the time the competition started, Ramsey had a team he felt could compete on an even footing with the rest of the world. He was counting on three advantages to put England over the top. First, his players had the home crowd behind them. Second, he had selected and trained a team that had learned how to adjust to anything a foreign team might throw at them; flexibility, as he saw it, was the x-factor when it came to winning the World Cup. And third, Ramsey employed an interesting new formation that pulled the wings back off the front line, creating a 2-4-4 alignment where the fullbacks could and often did overlap with the forwards.

Charlton was joined by defensive whiz Bobby Moore, talented winger Alan Ball, goalie Gordon Banks, and a late addition at forward named Geoff Hurst. The main challenge in World Cup '66, Ramsey knew, was likely to come from Brazil. Italy and the West German team, led by young halfback Franz Beckenbauer, were extremely dangerous, too. England got its first break when Brazil was put out by Portugal. Two rough tackles caused Pelé to leave the game, which enabled Eusebio to step up and score the final two goals in a shocking 3-1 victory. Italy, meanwhile, was ambushed by North Korea, whose fleet-footed forwards ran circles around the big burly defenders. It was the greatest victory ever for an Asian soccer team, though the Koreans almost outdid themselves in their next match, against Portugal. They stunned the crowd by scoring three goals in the first 22 minutes, and it took a miraculous performance by Eusebio to avert a major disaster for the Portuguese.

In the semifinals, West Germany, led by its beloved captain, Uwe Seeler, got by the Soviet Union, while England beat Portugal 2-1 on a pair of goals by Charlton. The final was a classic duel, with Helmut Haller opening the scoring and Hurst knotting the game 19 minutes into the first half. It remained 1-1 until, with 12 minutes to go, Martin Peters scored for England. But with time running out, Wolfgang Weber managed to bang one past Banks to send the game into extra time.

Eleven minutes into the period, Ball pushed a pass into the middle where Hurst, with his back to the net, controlled it and then quickly wheeled and fired. His shot hit the crossbar, ricocheted straight down and bounced out before anyone got a good look at whether the ball had actually crossed the goal line. After much arguing and a long conference by the referees, Hurst's shot was ruled a goal, giving England a 3-2 lead.

Hurst netted a third just before extra time expired to become the only player in history to achieve a hat trick in a World Cup final. England had its World Cup, just as Ramsey had predicted, and the country won back some much-needed soccer self-respect. After World Cup '66, many teams adopted Ramsey's 2-4-4 setup. From that point forward, wing play declined dramatically, while defensive alignments became more and more popular.

A New U.S. Pro League

Among the worldwide television audience for the 1966 World Cup final were 10 million Americans. Despite the U.S. team's failure to qualify for the tournament, interest in soccer seemed to be on the rise. On the way to the World Cup that spring, the Argentine

Bobby Moore (holding trophy) celebrates England's victory in the 1966 World Cup final with his coach and teammates.

and Brazilian teams stopped in Los Angeles to play an exhibition match, and 30,000 fans attended the game. After the World Cup, Santos and Benfica squared off in a special match at Randall's Island in New York. More than 40,000 showed up to see this epic clash between Pelé and Eusebio. The timing appeared to be right for a stab at creating a major soccer league in the United States.

In the fall of 1966, no less than two professional soccer leagues formed to capitalize on this growing interest. The United Soccer Association imported entire teams of foreign players and placed them in key cities. The National Professional Soccer League relied on a mix of American players with a sprinkling of over-the-hill foreign stars. Each was in a desperate race to win a television contract, but neither could draw the kind of crowds the networks liked to see. In 1967, both leagues folded, then reorganized as the North American Soccer League. The old ASL, which was still in operation, simply faded away.

World Cup '70

The 1970s will always be remembered as the decade when soccer truly went global. Tremendous amounts of money poured into the sport from television revenues, corporate sponsorships, player and club endorsements, and, of course, increased attendance. The fuse that ignited this soccer explosion was none other than Pelé, who returned to the international stage at World Cup '70 in Mexico. Injuries had twice robbed the Brazilian superstar of an opportunity to repeat the magical performance of 1958, and he and his teammates vowed that this would not happen again. In their favor, the style and caliber of officiating had evolved somewhat over the years to protect finesse players such as Pelé. No longer could brutish fullbacks slam smaller players to the ground and expect to get away with it.

Pelé had some help this time, too, in the person of Jairzinho, a marvelous attacking player who could pass and shoot as well as anyone in the world. He scored in each of Brazil's six matches at World Cup 1970, including a pivotal 1-0 victory over defending champion England. In that game, goalie Gordon Banks robbed Pelé of a goal with one of the greatest saves ever seen. Taking a high cross from Jairzinho, Pelé leaped into the air, faked Banks right, then headed a wicked bouncing ball toward the left post. Banks somehow twisted his body—seemingly going two directions at once—to tip the ball over the crossbar. In an earlier game, against Czechoslovakia, Pelé had nearly scored a goal from his own half of the field. If there is a category for all-time great near-misses, these two attempts would have to rank right at the top.

Another memorable performance was turned in by West German scoring machine Gerd Müller. Nicknamed *Der Bomber*, Müller was a squat, powerful center-forward who often looked out of place among the chiseled physiques of his teammates. But he possessed a sixth sense for where loose balls would be, and his powerful foot and accurate head enabled him to put through an astonishing 68 goals in 62 international matches during the 1960s and 1970s. Against the defensive-minded Italians, Müller was unstoppable, scoring twice in extra time. But it was Italy that prevailed, with three late goals of its own to reach the championship game.

In the final, Brazil attacked and Italy concentrated on defense, waiting for a mis-

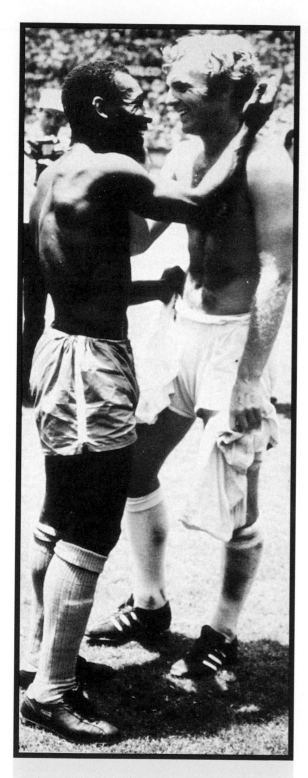

Brazil's Pelé and England's Bobby Moore exchange shirts after a World Cup match in 1970.

take. But mistakes were few and far between, for Brazil's was truly a team of superstars. Besides Pelé and Jairzinho, there were Tostao, Gerson, and Rivelino—each man easily ranking among the top 20 players in the world, and each had a compelling story. The light-skinned Tostao, whose given name was Eduardo Goncalves Andrade, was nicknamed the White Pelé for his similar build and playing style. A year earlier, he suffered a detached retina during a game and was only able to return to the field after a delicate operation performed in the United States. He retired in 1973 at the age of 26 for fear of doing permanent damage. He later became an eye doctor. Roberto Rivelino, who operated from the left wing, could work wonders with a soccer ball. He was not especially fast, nor was his shot particularly hard, but he could make the ball curve, dip, and bend in seemingly impossible ways. Where others saw a tangled mass of defenders in front of the goal, Rivelino saw a curved universe of open teammates and poorly positioned defenders.

Gerson, whose full name was Gerson Nunes de Oliveira, acted as the brain of this incredible front line. He was a master at sensing the development of scoring opportunities and was able to think right along with his four talented teammates. Prematurely bald, he looked like the team's wise old man. And it would take a wise man to beat the big, physical Italians, who played tight, in-your-face man-to-man defense.

In a classic contrast of styles, the free-flowing Brazilians probed the conservative Italian defense until things finally started to click. Pelé scored on a first-half header, then Gerson broke a 1-1 deadlock with a long goal in the 66th minute. Five minutes later, Gerson put a free kick on Pelé's head, and before the Italians could react he had directed it right on to Jairzinho's foot for an easy score. The final goal was another Pelé masterpiece, as he took a pass from Jairzinho, drew a crowd and then left it for halfback Carlos Alberto, who boomed it into the net. The 4-1 final score sent a strong message to the soccer world, which more and more had been favoring a strategy of containment over attack. The Italians, led by Alberto Boninsegna, could not have played better. The same could be said for Brazil, which was arguably the finest team ever to take the field.

The tournament itself also represented a high-water mark for soccer. In terms of overall quality and excitement, it was easily the best World Cup to that time and, few would argue, ever since. That most of the matches were played at midday under the blazing sun to accommodate European television made the stellar performances all the more remarkable.

An International Affair

With the decade off to a roaring start, soccer in Europe and the Americas flourished as never before. Fan interest continued to increase, but the focus of their affections had begun to change. The idea of a hero had become somewhat antiquated, part of an innocent world that began to crumble with worldwide student unrest during the late 1960s, the last gasp of European colonialism, and the Vietnam War. Heroes were now "superstars." Fans began to pull back on their loyalties for local and national teams and began to embrace players in other parts of the world. No one rooted against their own country in international matches—that

In Mexico City, Pelé holds up the Jules Rimet cup, which Brazil won after defeating Italy 4-1 in the 1970 World Cup final. It was the third time Brazil had won the cup, so under FIFA rules they were entitled to keep it.

would be suicidal—but many soccer aficionados expanded their views and moved toward a more global perspective.

The companies that pumped money into soccer picked up on this trend and began looking at players who could give their products—from shoes to equipment to soft drinks—an international presence. It was not unusual to see the face of an Italian star in a French magazine or the face of an Argentine star in a Swedish journal. Not surprisingly, the movement of players from one country to another increased dramatically. With the exception of English Football League followers, fans no longer cared if all of their favorite team's players were "local boys." They wanted to win, and they wanted the best talent available. More to the point, they knew who was available, whether they were playing in the next country or half a world away.

Among the players who were thrust into the spotlight during the early part of the decade were Franz Beckenbauer, Johan Cruyff, and Johan Neeskens.

Cruyff and Neeskens played for Holland's fabulous Ajax club, as well as the Dutch international team. They formed the backbone of what came to be called "total football," where all 10 players on a team possessed similar skills and could thus interchange positions at any time. This strategy had been attempted by Austria during the 1950s—it was called the Whirl back then—but it was Holland that finally pulled it off two decades later. Cruyff roamed the field at will from his center-forward position. One moment he would be cruising around midfield, and then he might turn up on the wing or drive down the middle. He drove defenses crazy and was one of the few players who could dominate a game for

long stretches. Cruyff was the best player in the world during this time, winning Footballer of the Year honors three times in four seasons.

Neeskens was more defensive-minded, yet he could be a dangerous offensive player, too. When the dramatic charges of Cruyff and cohorts Johnny Rep, Piet Keizer, and Wim Van Hanegem were turned back, it was the sharp-tackling Neeskens who stopped counterattacks before they got started. With Cruyff and Neeskens starring, Ajax won three straight European Cups from 1971 to 1973. In 1973, the Barcelona club purchased Cruyff—nearly doubling the previous record for a transfer fee—and Cruyff paid immediate dividends, leading the long-moribund team to the league title. Neeskens joined him there in 1974.

Beckenbauer was the oldest of the three, a veteran of two World Cups by the mid-1970s. An attacking player whose charges up the field brought fans to their feet, the cool and calculating "Kaiser Franz" was something new to the game: an offensive-minded sweeper. Beckenbauer patrolled midfield for the great Bayern Munich clubs of the 1970s, and twice he was voted European Footballer of the Year. Many felt his talents would have been better used on the front line, but European defenses were so tight at this time that he might not have had enough space to maneuver. Indeed, Beckenbauer much preferred trailing a play, analyzing the field, setting up teammates, and penetrating defenses himself when he saw an opening. In a span of nine years, Beckenbauer won the European Cup-Winners' Cup, the European Championship, the World Club Cup, and the European Cup. His biggest triumph,

JOHAN CRUYFF

Johan Cruyff, pictured here in his NASL jersey, won European Footballer of the Year three times.

For most players, soccer boils down to a game of survival. The potential gain of each option must be weighed, in a split second, against what might happen if something goes wrong. Even when the sport was more wide-open than today, these thoughts ran through the mind of virtually every player. Among the few exceptions, and certainly the most notable, was Johan Cruyff. To him, playing soccer was a quest for perfection.

Born in the Dutch city of Amsterdam, Cruyff played soccer and rooted for the Ajax club like most boys his age. Unlike other kids, however, Cruyff had an edge: his mother cleaned the club's offices, and she pestered team officials until they agreed to put him into their youth program at the age of 12. By age 17, he made the club, and at 19 he scored a goal in his first game for the Dutch national team.

Cruyff's offical position was center-forward, but he played everywhere—at midfield, on the wings, and even back in front of his own goal at times. He would spend an entire match roaming the pitch, probing for a weakness or a new angle of attack. Each game was an adventure for Cruyff and a nightmare for his opponents, who never knew where to look for him next. The Juventus players experienced Cruyff at his best during the 1972 European Cup final. He stretched them to the breaking point, swirling in and around the defense and scoring both goals in a 2-0 victory—the second of three straight European Cup titles for Ajax. In 1973, Cruyff transferred to the Barcelona club for a record fee. He took the team from the bottom of the standings to the league championship.

Inspired by Cruyff, a generation of excellent all-around soccer players emerged in Holland during the 1970s, enabling the national team to install a system that fans called "total football." Basically, it was a form of highly organized chaos designed to make other teams make mistakes. Each player on the club could move easily in and out of any position as situations dictated. It made the Dutch players hard to mark, and also made for some wonderful teamwork and passing on the field. Some believe soccer reached its pinnacle at this time.

Cruyff captained Holland to the World Cup final in 1974, then put in another spectacular season for Barcelona. In 1978, at the age of 31, he left Europe and signed a lucrative contract to play with the Los Angeles Aztecs in the NASL, and won the league MVP in his first season. In 1984, Cruyff returned to Ajax as technical director to find the team in shambles. Within three years, however, he guided his old club to the Cup-Winners' Cup championship, then took the manager's job at Barcelona, where he led the team to victory in the 1995 European Cup final.

FRANZ BECKENBAUER

By the end of the 1960s, soccer was undergoing a fundamental shift regarding the philosophy of how a team's best all-around performer should be used. The predominant theory had long been that such a player might be of greatest service at the center-halfback or center-forward position. But soccer was changing, becoming more of a defensive battle, so a player who could analyze the flow of a game was likely to be more useful as a defender than as a scorer. Still, anchoring a good offensive player to the back line made no sense, because his passing and shooting talents were also needed up front. From this quandary came the attacking sweeper solution, and a new position was created.

No player made the modern sweeper position work better than West Germany's Franz Beckenbauer. He alternated between playing behind his fullbacks as the last line of defense and playing up with the halfbacks, where he could double as an attacker. Skilled enough as a dribbler, passer, and shooter to play anywhere he pleased, Beckenbauer created major problems for opponents. And breakaways against his Bayern Munich club were few and far between, for "Kaiser Franz" was rarely caught too deep when play turned the other way.

Indeed, Beckenbauer claimed he could see openings on the field before they actually opened. On offense, when it appeared to fans that he was dribbling toward a congested part of the field, it would miraculously spread out just prior to his arrival. On defense, opponents would launch what looked like a dangerous attack, then someone would inexplicably put the ball right on Beckenbauer's foot. Knowledgeable fans knew this was a tribute to his tremendous anticipation and computer-like soccer mind.

Beckenbauer started for Bayern Munich in 1964 as a teenager and made the national team in 1965. At World Cup '66, he helped the West German squad make it to the final. It was the following year that he moved to sweeper, and by season's end he had led the team to the Cup-Winners' Cup title from that position.

For most of the 1970s Beckenbauer was regarded as the supreme player in European soccer. He was named Footballer of the Year in 1972 and 1976 and engineered West Germany's World Cup championship in 1974. Beckenbauer joined the New York Cosmos of the NASL. He instantly transformed the team, leading New York to the NASL championship three times in four seasons.

Although a magnificent athlete, Beckenbauer's greatest attribute was his soccer mind. As manager of West Germany's national team, he coaxed a superstar performance out of a solid but unspectacular bunch at World Cup '86, guiding them all the way to the final. And in 1990, he became the first person to captain one World Cup winner and then manage another when West Germany defeated Argentina 1-0 in the final.

however, came when he led his country into World Cup '74.

World Cup '74

As host country, West Germany was fully expected to win. But knowledgeable fans feared the Dutch and Polish teams with their "controlled chaos" offenses that were capable of scoring at any time even against the most conservative defenses. This proved true early on as the Poles, bolstered by their gold-medal performance in the 1972 Olympics, beat both Argentina and Italy to win their group and make the quarterfinals. Led by Kazimierz Deyna and Robert Gadocha and backed up by goalie Jan Tomaszewski, Poland continued its charge toward the final by disposing of the Swedish and Yugoslavian teams as well. It took the powerful West Germans to finally stop them, and this they did by the slimmest of margins in a 1-0 nail-biter won by Gerd Müller. The other half of the tournament saw Holland sweep to the final, allowing just one goal in five matches. Soccer fans squirmed in anticipation, as once again a clash of two divergent strategies would decide the World Cup champion.

In a shocking start, the score was 1-0 before a German player ever touched the ball. The Dutch took the opening kickoff and worked the ball into Cruyff, who was creamed inside the penalty box. Neeskens buried the penalty kick and that was that. Outplayed and, at times, overwhelmed, the West Germans caught a huge break when Bernd Holzenbein was taken down in front of the Dutch goal, and Paul Breitner rammed home the penalty kick for a 1-1 tie. One minute before halftime, Gerd Müller squeezed off an unstoppable shot from the top of the penalty area for his record-setting 14th career World Cup goal and a precarious 2-1 lead. The second half was as exciting and intense as the first, with one important exception: neither team scored. It was a clear triumph for West Germany's efficient, calculating style. But the game also introduced the world to a brand of soccer that many would emulate but no one would ever really perfect.

Stars of the Seventies

World Cup heroes Breitner and Deyna were among the many emerging stars of the early 1970s. Breitner was a smart, hard-tackling

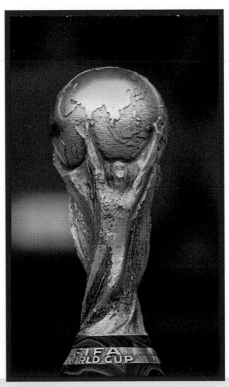

The World Cup trophy is the prize sought by soccer players worldwide.

left fullback for Bayern Munich, who played his very best in the big games against the most dangerous forwards. He was not a fan of the slow-moving German style of play and later transferred to Real Madrid, where he moved up to halfback and had a brilliant career. This did not exactly endear him to the German national team, which left him off the 1978 World Cup roster. Breitner returned to the team for World Cup '82 and became one of only four players ever to score goals in two World Cup finals.

Deyna was the centerpiece of the Polish attack in the early 1970s and a big reason for the country's gold medal in Munich in 1972. From his position at center-half, he distributed the ball to talented strikers like Gadocha and Grzegorz Lato, and he could also come up and score himself when the opportunity arose. Deyna left Poland after the 1974 World Cup, going first to Manchester United and then to the NASL in America, where he died in a car crash.

A couple of East German players made soccer news during the 1970s despite playing behind the Iron Curtain. Hans-Jürgen Dorner of Dynamo Dresden was one of the top defensive players in the game, an enforcer who could scare opponents out of the penalty area with just a glance. He was equally effective when assuming the sweeper role, winning East German Footballer of the Year three times, leading Dynamo Dresden to five league championships and playing a key part in his country's gold medal at the 1976 Olympics. Dorner's national teammate, and star of the Magdeburg club, was Jürgen Sparwasser, an attacking midfielder who scored the goal that beat West Germany in the third game of World Cup '74—the one and only meeting between these teams in 40 years. Sparwasser

also keyed Magdeburg's 1974 victory over AC Milan in the final of the European - Cup-Winners' Cup. A few years later, he defected during a tournament in West Germany.

Great Britain produced a pair of top players, too, in Kenny Dalglish and Kevin Keegan. Dalglish, a Scotsman who started with the Celtic club in Glasgow during the late 1960s, became a valuable performer with a gift for spotting opportunity and the ability to concentrate regardless of what tactics opponents employed to stop him. At age 19, he helped the team to the 1970 European Cup final and got them back to the semifinals in 1972. In 1974, Dalglish was sold for 400,000 pounds to Liverpool, where he became one of the world's most highly respected players, leading the team to three European Cup titles in four years. There he teamed briefly with Keegan, who in 1977 transferred to the Hamburg club in West Germany.

Keegan was a smart, tough, charismatic little forward who could rally a team around him. He was also the finest finisher of his time, rarely missing a scoring chance. Keegan had all the goods: he possessed a strong foot, could dribble almost as fast as he could run, could spring into the air, and he could slice through the tiniest of openings. Keegan powered Liverpool to the FA Cup, the European Cup, and a pair of UEFA Cups during his six years with the team; then he led Hamburg to the top of the German league for the first time in 19 years. He was named European Footballer of the Year twice in the late 1970s.

South America also turned out a couple of players good enough to move out of the shadow cast by Brazil's band of veteran stars. Carlos Caszely was a high-scoring and outspoken inside-forward for the Colo Colo club in Chile, which he led to the finals of the Copa Libertades in 1973. That same year, President Allende was overthrown, and Caszely's political views got him into hot water with the new conservative government. He transferred to the Levante club in Spain, where he became one of Europe's top scoring threats, then returned to anchor Chile's World Cup entries in 1974 and 1982. Mario Kempes was even more dangerous around the goal. The Argentine star had legs like sledgehammers, as he would prove against Holland in the 1978 World Cup final. Like Caszely, he transferred to a Spanish club, Valencia, where he developed so impressively that he was the only Argentine-born player in Europe recalled to the national team in 1978.

Despite the considerable allure of Spain's foreign-born stars, its most popular player during this era was probably José Martinez Sanchez, who went by the nickname Pirri. He evolved from an opportunistic scorer into a valuable defender during his 15 years with Real Madrid, during which he won eight Spanish championships. After retiring in 1979 he completed his medical studies and returned to his old team as club doctor.

With defensive play the focus in much of the world during the 1970s, goalies were asked to handle fewer quality shots. Still, the big save retained its importance as a momentum-shifter, and goalies who could anticipate and react to developing attacks remained a top commodity. Four goalies active during the early part of the decade stood out. The best of the bunch was Sepp Maier, who in 1974 won the European Cup with Bayern Munich and minded the nets for West Germany's World Cup victory. Like

most of the men who play the position, he was something of a character, known for his long shorts and his love of tennis. Dino Zoff was Italy's top goalie during the 1970s, playing for Juventus and also the national team. In 1973–74, he went 1,134 minutes without allowing a goal in international play, and in 1982, he was in the net for Italy's World Cup championship.

Perfection was something of an obsession for England's Peter Shilton, who was as fanatical about his physical training as he was about eliminating mistakes. His finest hour as a pro came in 1977–78 with Nottingham Forest, which had clawed its way out of the Second Division the season before. With Shilton shoring up an already-tough defense, Forest went all the way to the top of the standings that year. In international competition, Shilton was a rare four-decade player, making his first appearance for England in 1969 and getting his final cap in World Cup '90. Another ironman from the British Isles was Pat Jennings of Northern Ireland, who played more than 1,000 matches in his 24-year career. He participated in four FA Cup finals and once scored a goal against Manchester United in a charity game.

The stars who carried the game into the 1970s were a fine group. Still, it was with great sadness that the soccer world bid farewell to Pelé, who announced his retirement in 1974. Behind his wonderful play, Brazil had won the World Cup three times. And it was he who awakened the world to the beauty of the South American game. Pelé was still the best player in the world, but at age 33 it just seemed like a good time to call it quits and enjoy himself. Of course, he could not simply turn off the adoration of millions of fans; Pelé was the most famous athlete in the world. Everywhere he went, he was instantly recognized and mobbed by adoring fans. Everywhere, that is, except the United States.

The NASL

In the United States, soccer was still struggling to gain a foothold. The early 1970s saw encouraging growth in high school and college soccer programs, and dozens of semipro leagues were thriving across the country. The NASL was making a go of it, too, despite a very shaky start. In 1968, the league boasted 17 teams, a television contract with CBS, and a small but enthusiastic fan base. By 1970, twelve teams had folded, and CBS had pulled the plug on the TV deal. Still, the league limped forward, concentrating less on signing foreign players and more on selling soccer to kids and educating adult fans in the markets the NASL occupied.

Recognizing the U.S. sports fan's appetite for statistics, the league awarded players two points for a goal and one for an assist—a stat that was not even kept in most parts of the world. Furthermore, teams would get six points for a win, three for a tie and one point for each goal scored, up to three. This gave teams something to shoot for even when a game seemed to be decided, and it gave fans all sorts of mathematical possibilities to calculate as the season neared its climax. There were six teams—Atlanta, Kansas City, San Diego, Rochester, Dallas, and Washington, D.C.—in the league in 1970. The following year, that number swelled to eight, as Kansas City dropped out and new teams were added in Montreal, Toronto, and, importantly, New York. The NASL added another wrinkle by scheduling games with foreign clubs, such as Apollo of Greece and Brazilian power

Portuguese Rio, and counting the results in the standings.

In 1972, the New York Cosmos won the NASL championship. The league needed a successful team in New York. Although the team's home field on Randall's Island was difficult to get to and fans were usually outnumbered by the island's spectacularly large rats, it still looked good to have a New York team at the top of the standings. In 1973, the Philadelphia Atoms joined the league. Their team was made up mostly of American-born players from the college ranks, including goalie Bob Rigby, former All-American Casey Bahr, and Barry Barto, the star of the Philadelphia Textile team. By sprinkling in a few colorful Englishmen, including Andy "The Flea" Provan, the Atoms really connected with their fans and averaged more than 11,000 spectators per game.

The NASL title game that year pitted the

Goalie Shep Messing was one of the few U.S.-born stars to play in the NASL. His unconventional personality made him a fan favorite.

GENDER EQUITY

In 1979, Congress passed the law known as Title IX, which essentially guaranteed that no one could be denied access to high school or college athletic programs based on gender. At that time, there was a grand total of 17 women's collegiate soccer programs. Today, there are more than 700, making women's soccer the fastest growing sport on college campuses. This participation explosion has also catapulted the U.S. women's team to the top of international soccer and made household names of such stars as Mia Hamm and Michelle Akers. At the 1996 Olympic Games, the U.S. team overpowered opponents to take the gold medal.

In a fascinating twist of irony, many soccer insiders believe that Title IX may one day prove to be the turning point in the *men's* game. Today's female players are tomorrow's moms, and they are very likely to steer their sons away from football, baseball, and track and into the game they themselves played as teenagers. This would give American soccer a much-needed infusion of the top athletes it has traditionally lost to those other sports.

U.S. star Mia Hamm controls a pass during the 1996 Olympics women's soccer finals. The United States won the first Olympic gold medal ever awarded in women's soccer.

Three girls battle for control of the ball during a youth league game. Many women worldwide play soccer, and in the United States women's soccer is the fastest growing sport on college campuses.

Atoms against the Dallas Tornado, which featured Kyle Rote, Jr., the first American soccer player whose name was familiar to fans outside the sport. Kyle Rote, Sr., had been an All-American football star in Dallas at Southern Methodist University and went on to have a great career with the NFL New York Giants. During the 1970s he was a nationally known sports commentator, and this generated much recognition and publicity for his son, and therefore the league. The 1973 "Soccer Bowl" was won by Philadelphia 2-0, marking the first time a team had ever captured a major professional championship in the United States during its first year of existence.

Although still financially strapped, the NASL owners could finally see the light at the end of the tunnel. Big crowds could be drawn for games—18,000 had attended the 1973 NASL final in Dallas—and the right kind of stars could reach out beyond the soccer world and potentially pull in millions of fans. They were convinced that soccer could finally be sold to Americans as a legitimate big-time sport. Indeed, international soccer coverage was beginning to find its way into the U.S. mainstream, in magazines like *Sports Illustrated* and in the sports sections of many newspapers. Slowly but surely, the names of the world's top players—Müller, Eusebio, Cruyff, Chinaglia, and Beckenbauer—were becoming more familiar to baseball, football, and basketball fans every day.

The man Americans most closely associated with soccer was still Pelé, who was winding up his brilliant career in Brazil. When he announced his retirement in 1974, he left behind records that boggled the mind: three World Cup wins, 127 goals in a season (1959) and 1,088 career goals. But he was far

from finished. The one place where he had failed to leave an impression was the United States, and this intrigued him. Eight months after hanging up his boots, Pelé signed what was then the largest contract in pro sports history, a three-year $4.75 million dollar deal to play for the New York Cosmos.

If anyone could make soccer work in the United States, it would be Pelé. In his first game, which was broadcast nationally by ABC, he scored a goal and set up another in an exhibition win over Kyle Rote Jr.'s Dallas

Pelé awaits a pass from a New York Cosmos teammate. Pelé came out of retirement and joined the NASL to help establish professional soccer in the United States.

Stars. The ratings for the game were excellent, and the NASL seemed on its way.

By 1975, the league had expanded to 19 teams, and with Pelé as the circuit's big box-office attraction, attendance swelled and enough money was flowing in that other franchises could afford to start signing big-name foreign players. Over the next few years, George Best and Johan Cruyff agreed to play for the Los Angeles Aztecs, Gerd Müller went to the Ft. Lauderdale Strikers, the Boston Minutemen signed Eusebio, the San Diego Sockers lured Kazimierz Deyna, and Tampa Bay inked English First Division standouts Rodney Marsh, Stewart Scullion, Clyde Best, and Derek Smethurst. The Cosmos, playing to huge crowds, used the financial windfall created by Pelé's presence to surround him with a team of all-time greats, including the Dutch star Neeskens and Giorgio Chinaglia of Italy.

Most of these players were slightly past their primes but still possessed great skill. They liked the wide-open NASL game, which favored shooting, passing, and finesse. Here they believed they could showcase their skills in a way that was more understandable for U.S. fans.

The first superstar to join the NASL in his prime was Franz Beckenbauer, who inked a deal with the Cosmos in 1976 after winning his second European Footballer of the Year award. Beckenbauer joined a team that was being called the best money could buy, but when he arrived late in May the Cosmos had won just one more game than they had lost. New York's coach, Gordon Bradley, was popular with the players but had failed to maximize the talent he put on the field. His use of Beckenbauer as a sweeper, for instance, ignored the fact that the offside rule in the NASL was dramatically different than in Europe, where players were compelled to retreat only past the midfield line when on defense. In the NASL, the offside line was just 35 yards from the goal, meaning counterattacks—a Beckenbauer specialty—often had to be launched from much farther back. The Kaiser could still move his team up the field, but by starting so far back he could not do it as often or effectively as he had while playing in Germany.

Bradley was replaced by Eddie Firmani in early July, and the first thing he did was move Beckenbauer to the midfield position, where he would have to cover less distance. Next he obtained the service of fullback Carlos Alberto, the captain of Pelé's 1970 World Cup team. The move paid immediate dividends, as the Cosmos advanced through the playoffs to the Soccer Bowl, where they beat the Seattle Sounders 2-1. Along the way, the Cosmos drew a crowd of 77,691 to the Meadowlands for a second-round game against the Ft. Lauderdale Strikers. As Pelé walked away from the game in the United States, it seemed to be on its way. Indeed, the Cosmos continued their dominance over the next few years, winning the NASL championship again in 1978 and 1980, regularly drawing big crowds both at home and on the road.

World Cup '78

The buildup for World Cup '78 was, in many ways, much more interesting than the actual tournament. According to the experts, this was to be the year when Holland would assert its dominance and alter forever the way soccer was played. In the four years since World Cup '74, Dutch players had all but perfected the wheeling, free-form offense that had so captivated fans in the early

1970s. The host country, Argentina, was the other favorite, although their road to the final would include severe tests against talented teams from Italy, Brazil, and Poland.

The Argentine fans put on a show, cheering wildly throughout games and regularly showering the field with tickertape. Their team, however, was not as impressive. They beat Hungary in the opening game only after two opposing players had been sent off and then lost to Italy 1-0. Only a tight win over the French got Argentina to the quarterfinals. The early surprise of the World Cup was Tunisia, which beat Mexico and battled the astonished West Germans to a scoreless tie. It marked the first time an African country had made a major impact in the tournament. Had Tunisia converted one of its many scoring opportunities against the Germans, they would have bumped them out of the tournament.

The best game of the World Cup pitted West Germany against Holland in a semifinal replay of their 1974 meeting. Holland needed only a tie to make it to the final, and this it achieved as the Germans were unable to break a 2-2 deadlock. In the other semifinal, Argentina needed to beat Peru by four goals to unseat Brazil, which had eliminated Poland in convincing fashion. With a capacity crowd in River Plate Stadium cheering them on, the Argentines got a pair of goals from their star, Kempes, and beat Peru easily—too easily, some claimed—to earn a spot in the final. Rumors persist to this day that the Peruvians did not put forth their best effort in this match, tarnishing the entire tournament.

The Argentina-Holland final was not what most soccer fans had been rooting for, but the game was a dramatic one. Kempes scored for the attacking Argentines, and Dirk Nanninga scored the equalizer for the Dutchmen with nine minutes left. Incredibly, Nanninga had predicted to reporters he would score, even though he was a substitute who did not figure to play much. Dutch star Rob Rensenbrink appeared to win the game when he blasted a shot past Argentina's Ubaldo Fillol in the last minute of regulation time, but the ball hit the post and caromed away. After 90 minutes, the score stood at 1-1. In extra time, Kempes beat three Dutch defenders to make the score 2-1, then Daniel Bertoni scored the final goal and Argentina had its first World Cup.

New Stars

As the decade turned, soccer received an important boost when FIFA announced that the final field for World Cup '82 would be expanded from 16 to 24 teams. Countries that had never held out much hope for a World Cup berth suddenly had eight more places to shoot for, and fan interest in those countries increased dramatically. Also, because of the increased likelihood that they would soon be performing on the world stage, the top players from such non-powers as Cameroon, Algeria, Honduras, and New Zealand drew more attention than ever before.

A new group of young stars emerged in the late 1970s that would take soccer into the 1980s. Some of them came from familiar places and some did not, confirming the steady spread of world-class play across the entire globe. Cha Bum Kun, South Korea's best player, left his country to test his skills against the world's finest footballers in 1978 and was treated as a traitor by his people. Cha starred for three teams in the West German league from 1978 to 1986, when he was finally coaxed back to play for South Korea's World Cup squad. Roger Milla emerged as a top player for Cameroon, winning African Footballer of the Year in 1976 and then moving on to France. There he helped Monaco win the league title in 1980 and did the same for Bastia in 1981. A charming character who delighted fans with his on-field enthusiasm, Milla was all business when he bore down on opposing goalies from his center-forward position.

Argentina continued to produce excellent players after its World Cup win. Team captain Daniel Passarella blossomed into an international superstar with the Fiorentina club in Italy, becoming one of the top central defenders of modern times. Halfback Jorge Valdano, who left Argentina as a teenager for political reasons, carved out a brilliant career with the Alaves, Zaragoza, and Real Madrid clubs in Spain before returning home as a key ingredient in Argentina's 1986 World Cup run. Valdano was a thinking-man's player and a thinking man, to boot. He was an author and poet, and when his career ended prematurely after a bout with hepatitis, he became a celebrated journalist, broadcast analyst, and coach.

The top player developed by Argentina—and the top player of his time—was Diego Maradona. Around him swirled both magic and controversy, as well as cold, hard cash. A nationally known prodigy by the age of 15, Maradona was sold for a record price three times between 1980 and 1984, moving from Argentina to Barcelona and eventually to Naples, where he put in seven remarkable seasons. He could dribble around gangs of defenders and thread magnificent passes to streaking teammates. His talented left foot could blast a rocket shot through the slimmest of openings or curl the ball to any part of the goal. An instinctive,

Youngsters play soccer in an African town. Soccer is the world's most popular sport.

aggressive player who seemed to be in the thick of every important play, Maradona was worshiped by fans on two continents.

France produced its most impressive player since 1958 World Cup hero Just Fontaine in the person of Michel Platini. After distinguishing himself in the 1976 Olympics and the 1978 World Cup tournament, he became France's top player and produced a heroic performance at World Cup '82. Sold to Juventus at the age of 27, he led the Italian league in scoring three times and led his club to the European Cup in 1985. He is the only player ever to win European Footballer of the Year honors three times in a row. Other notables from the late 1970s and early 1980s include Austria's Hans Krankl, who won the prestigious Golden Boot award in 1978 as Europe's top scorer, and West Germany's Karl-Heinz Rummenigge, who was named Footballer of the Year in 1980 and 1981 for Bayern Munich. Injuries limited Rummenigge's effectiveness after that, but he still commanded a multimillion dollar transfer fee when he went from Munich to Italy's Internazionale club in 1984.

From the British Isles came a pair of noteworthy performers. Midfielder Graeme Souness starred for Liverpool and the Sampdoria club in Italy and distinguished himself as a star in 50-plus international matches. Sammy McIlroy, from Northern Ireland, was another world-class midfielder. Always moving, always looking for action, McIlroy went to three FA Cup finals with Manchester United and represented his country in international play for 15 years.

Three world-class stars emerged from behind the Iron Curtain during this period. Oleg Blokhin possessed Olympic-caliber sprinting speed but chose instead to pursue a soccer career with Russia's Kiev Dynamo club. At 22, he led Kiev to the European Cup-Winners' Cup, pulling down Footballer of the Year honors in the process. In the late 1970s and early 1980s, Blokhin switched from left halfback to central striker and eventually was allowed to leave the Soviet Union and finish his career in Austria. Zbigniew Boniek came up on the heels of the exciting Polish teams of the 1970s and quickly developed into the greatest player his country ever produced. He did his best work as a member of the Juventus club, contributing mightily to its Cup-Winners' and European Cup victories in the mid-1980s. Center forward Zdenek Nehoda rose to prominence with Czechoslovakia's Dukla Prague club, twice winning his country's Footballer of the Year award. He later starred for teams in West Germany, Belgium, and Switzerland.

The era's most intriguing group of young players developed in Italy. Giancarlo Antognoni was the senior member of the group, having achieved superstar status for the Fiorentina club during the late 1970s. Bruno Conti was a talented right wing at a time when wing play was not considered key to a team's success. He was 25 before his career truly blossomed. Marco Tardelli was a midfielder with Juventus and other Italian clubs during the late 1970s and 1980s, and he distinguished himself as a big-play defender in league and international matches. Finally, there was Paolo Rossi, who timed the ups of his up-and-down career perfectly. Given away by Juventus as a teenager, he developed into a great scorer and eventually commanded a record transfer fee. Rossi was already a household name in Italy by World Cup '78 but became an international news story when he was implicated in a massive betting scandal that rocked the soccer world. The two-year suspension with which he was hit would have shattered most players, but Rossi picked up right where he left off, rejoining Juventus and winning Footballer of the Year in 1982. These four players, along with veteran goalkeeper Dino Zoff, were the heart of the national team that entered World Cup '82 as 14-1 underdogs.

World Cup '82

The smart money was on the West Germans, with Rummenigge leading a talented cast of characters, and Argentina, which had added Maradona to its cup-winning team of 1978. The Brazilians appeared to be back on track, too, with Zico, Junior, Socrates, and Toninho Cerezo. It seemed a certainty that two of these teams would meet in the final.

With 24 participating countries, a world-wide television audience, and commercial sponsorship at an all-time high, World Cup '82 looked very different from its predecessors. But it felt different, too. The world had had a tough four years, and in many ways it cast a shadow over the proceedings in sunny Barcelona. Argentina and England were engaged in a seemingly senseless war over the Falkland Islands; the Soviet Union had invaded Afghanistan; and Iran had made hostage-taking an international obsession. Ronald Reagan and Pope John Paul II had survived assassination attempts; Egyptian president Anwar Sadat had not. Once the matches got going, however, all seemed forgotten. World Cup '82 would not be a cure for the world's ills, but it would do just fine as a temporary painkiller.

There was the usual excitement created by early upsets, including a 2-1 Algerian victory over the West Germans in the opening game. England started like a house afire, sweeping aside the French, Czechoslovakian, and Kuwaiti teams to advance to Phase 2. Italy could not win any of its three opening games, tying Poland, Peru, and Cameroon in each. Only by the slimmest of margins—a single goal differential—did the Italians advance. With Argentina and Brazil in one group, along with Italy, the South American half of the final seemed assured, as the winner would likely play (and beat) Poland or the Soviets in the semifinals. On the other side, West Germany had only England and France blocking its path.

The West Germans did indeed make it to the finals, but not without an epic semifinal overtime battle against the French that was ultimately decided by penalty kicks. The other finalist was a shocker. Italy edged Argentina 2-1 and then used a Rossi hat trick to stun the Brazilians 3-2. Zoff then shut out the Poles—with Rossi adding two more goals—to set up a most unlikely showdown between the West Germans and Italians.

Italy hung on for dear life in a first half that did not feature one shot on goal by either side, including an embarrassing missed penalty kick by Antonio Cabrini. Then, in the second half, the long game against France began to wear on the West Germans. Tardelli and Conti stepped up their counter-attacking games for Italy, and Rossi scored to break the ice in what ended up an easy 3-1 victory and a fitting end to a storybook performance. The World Cup had never been a place where longshots came in, but the Italian team that hoisted the trophy was far better than the one that opened the tournament. As they had each done individually during their careers, the key players put it all together as a team at just the right time.

A Dark Cloud with a Silver Lining

For the eighth time in a row, the United States failed to qualify for the World Cup. Despite the fact that American soccer had its own professional league, with good coaching and an established infrastructure, the team that played for one of the 24 berths was disorganized and ill-prepared in its qualifying games. Sadly, this would be the situation throughout most of the decade, as the U.S. fell short again for World Cup '86.

Paolo Rossi scores a goal for Italy during its 1982 World Cup final against West Germany. Italy went on to win 3-1 and capture its third World Cup.

To the utter astonishment of everyone involved in soccer, interest in the game as a major sport was slowly dying in the United States. The NASL could not keep up the momentum it had achieved in the 1970s, and attendance frittered away to a few thousand a game—not nearly enough to support the escalating salary demands of top players. Even when the Players Association agreed to a salary cap, it only delayed the inevitable. In 1985, the league suspended operations. Giorgio Chinaglia purchased the Cosmos and tried to run the team as an independent entity, scheduling exhibition matches with top clubs from other countries. The end of this scheme came during a poorly attended game against Lazio of Italy at Giants Stadium when frustrated players engaged in an all-out brawl right on the field. After that, it seemed unlikely that pro soccer would thrive in the United States for a long, long time.

The problem was not that people had stopped playing. On the contrary, millions of kids, from grade school through college, loved the game. The problem was that no one was watching. In short, mainstream America still did not "get" soccer. There were a lot of theories as to why this was. The most plausible held that, to appreciate a sport, one has to have an understanding of what is happening when "nothing" is happening. If one has never played a sport—which in soccer's case was true of most older American sports fans—then it is impossible to understand the strategy and tension bubbling just beneath the surface. And without this understanding, it is hard to appreciate anything but the monotony of a 1-0 game.

Those who bemoaned the failure of soccer in the 1980s did have something to boost their spirits, however. They could look to the 1990s and beyond and know that millions of potential fans would possess the appreciation for soccer that was so lacking in the 1980s, because they would have grown up playing the game. But would they possess the *understanding* of soccer? The vast majority of soccer coaches in the United States were parents and gym teachers, themselves not well-schooled in the nuances of the game. Indeed, Europeans visiting the country during the early 1980s were unimpressed by the long-term implications of soccer's youth boom for this very reason. Even so, where the NASL had failed, another professional league might some day succeed. Add to this a growing immigrant population in the United States, and it was not hard to envision a much stronger fan base a decade or two down the line.

Ironically, the only professional segment of the sport that had developed a steady following in the 1980s was the Major Indoor Soccer League, which featured a six-on-six game it billed as "human pinball." For most soccer fans, the mere thought of the MISL was horrifying. Not only was it played in the cramped confines of a hockey rink, it eliminated most of the things they loved most about the game. But to Americans, it made a lot more sense. There was more scoring, more action, more substitutions, and plenty of timeouts. There was even a penalty box. The MISL officially arrived in 1983, when the St. Louis Steamers outbid the NASL Cosmos for the services of Rick Davis, the top American player and captain of the U.S. national team.

The college game was perhaps the most encouraging aspect of American soccer in the 1980s. It had come a long way since the first NCAA championship was held in 1959. The players and coaching were better, the scholarships were more plentiful, and the

In the late 1980s, Brazilian forward Tatu (left) and Yugoslav forward Preki (right) were two stars of the Major Indoor Soccer League.

level of competition was much higher than it had been even in the 1970s. Some feel that what really killed the NASL was the lack of good American college players. During the first ten years the league was in operation, the typical college star coming to the NASL could not compete with even the most marginal European and Latin American players. But there was no denying that quality and enthusiasm at the college level were on the rise.

By the close of the decade, two important events were to change the outlook for soccer in the United States. The first was the soccer competition at the Los Angeles Olympics in 1984, for which the rule banning professionals had been changed. Pros were now welcome to compete, as long as they had not appeared in the World Cup. This, coupled with the Soviet boycott of the games, led to an entertaining competition that featured some of the world's top young stars playing wide open soccer before enthusiastic American audiences. France took the gold medal—which for the first time in years was considered a meaningful achievement—beating Brazil 2-0 before 101,000 fans in the final. The second, and most important, moment for American soccer during the decade came in 1988, when FIFA awarded World Cup '94 to the United States.

World Cup '86

With the level of talent so high in the 1980s and so many great players on so many different teams, it seemed impossible for the World Cup to become a one-man show, as it had been when Pelé burst upon the scene in 1958. But soccer is a game of superstars and surprises. Even when all of the world's talent is concentrated in a single tournament, there is always that chance that one player will rise above the rest and carry his team to victory after victory. That, perhaps, is the best way to explain what happened at World Cup '86. Of course, what happened in Mexico that summer can also be explained with a single word: Maradona.

Eight months after a killer earthquake rocked Mexico City, Argentina's Diego Maradona came to town and shook the soccer world with an unforgettable performance. In the opener against South Korea, Maradona was fouled repeatedly. Yet each time he got up and stung his opponents, with trick plays, free kicks, and perfect passes. Against Italy, his long pass to Valdano accounted for the lone goal in a 1-1 tie. In the quarterfinals, Argentina faced England's strongest World Cup squad since 1966—a team that was pegged as an early favorite to reach the final. Adding to the pre-game tension was the fact that this was the first meeting between the two countries since the Falklands War. Six minutes into the second half, midfielder Steve Hodge lifted a back pass to his goalie, Peter Shilton. Maradona raced in and leaped high in the air to try and head the ball before Shilton could control it. The ball went in the goal, but it went in off Maradona's hand. The referee did not see it, and the play stood despite the wild protest of the English players. Asked later how the ball

managed to go in, Maradona said it must have been guided by the "hand of god." English fans still shudder at the mere mention of this play.

Four minutes later, the divine hand was apparently at work again when Maradona brought the ball out of his own end and began to head upfield. A 180-degree spin move left two defenders dead in their tracks, then he raced past a third man and headed down the right side and into enemy territory. Maradona drew another body at the top of the penalty area but twisted away and continued toward Shilton, who came out to cut down the angle. Maradona swerved around the English goal keeper and poked the ball into the open net as a sixth defender slid beneath him in a last-ditch effort to stop the unstoppable. Considered the most spectacular individual effort in World Cup history, Maradona's goal has been replayed countless times in every country in the world.

In the semifinals, Maradona scored both goals versus Belgium, including one that was only slightly less impressive than his second goal against England. West Germany prevailed against France in the other semifinal, shutting down Platini in a rematch of their 1982 overtime classic. In the final, Argentina established a 2-0 lead 10 minutes into the second half on a goal by Valdano. The Germans battled back in the last 20 minutes on two perfect corner kicks by Andy Brehme. The first was headed in by the captain, Rummenigge; the second was headed to wide-open substitute Rudi Völler, who directed it into the net. To that point, Maradona had been a factor only in that he had occupied one or two West German defenders for the entire game. They were determined not to let him beat them. But with the match heading toward extra time,

DIEGO MARADONA

In the late 1980s and early 1990s, the face of soccer greatness belonged to Diego Maradona. He possessed as much, or more, natural ability as anyone who ever played soccer. By the age of 16, he was a professional star. And at 17 he made the national team. Maradona was short, stocky and very, very fast. He could control the ball with his feet flawlessly, and he used this outrageous ability to make crowds leaping out of their seats by dribbling through entire teams to score magnificent goals.

With Maradona's artistic skills, however, came an artist's demeanor. He was impulsive, short-tempered, self-centered, and tempestuous. His critics said he was a selfish player who would not achieve true greatness until he learned how to think of himself as part of a team. When his ejection for a stupid foul against Brazil led to Argentina's early exit at World Cup '82, the chorus of criticism only grew louder. After the tournament, Maradona left South America and transferred to the Barcelona club for $10 million. When he transferred to Naples of the Italian league, Maradona finally began to pull his game together.

By World Cup '86, he had improved his team play to the point where Argentina was given a decent chance of reaching the final. By the end of the tournament, Maradona had propelled Argentina to the championship almost single-handedly. Though constantly double-teamed, he dribbled right through the slimmest openings, and many of the goals he scored probably could not have been scored by anyone else.

Maradona led Naples to league championships in 1987 and 1990. By World Cup '90, he was the most famous athlete in the world. Maradona was triple-teamed during most of the games, and though he failed to record a single goal during the competition, he did contribute immeasurably to Argentina's success. So much attention was focused on Maradona that his teammates were often left open. And they put the ball in the net just enough to return to the final, where they succumbed to West Germany.

After reaching the summit of soccer stardom, Maradona began a dramatic tumble. In 1991, he failed a drug test and was banned from Italian soccer and then was arrested for drug possession in Argentina, which led to a 15-month worldwide ban. When Maradona returned to soccer he wasn't nearly the dominant figure he had once been.

Diego Maradona splits two Greek defenders during a World Cup '94 match.

Romario holds up the Brazilian flag during the postgame celebrations of Brazil's victory over Sweden in a World Cup '94 match.

Maradona got the ball in his own end with nobody on him. As the Germans rushed to cut him off, he noticed Jorge Burruchaga standing all alone at midfield. Maradona blooped the ball over his helpless opponents and right to his teammate, who was off to the races. He blasted the ball past goalie Harald Schumacher and Argentina had its second World Cup.

The Seoul Games

Soccer took another important stride in 1988, during the Olympic competition in Seoul, South Korea. The gold medal was won by the Soviet Union, but the games were most notable for the many top-flight stars who suited up. For so many years, Olympic soccer had been little more than a playoff between Communist countries, whose players were listed as students, soldiers, and government workers, but who in reality were experienced professionals. Now, clearly, the Olympics were a suitable interlude to the World Cup, showcasing the talents of players, coaches, and national teams on the rise.

The country that grabbed the headlines at the Seoul games was Zambia, which stunned Italy 4-0 in a match that still has Italian fans muttering to themselves. The player who took the world's breath away with his inspired play at Seoul was a young Brazilian attacker named Romario. It was largely due to his brilliance that Brazil reached the final, and it was his astounding goal in that final that won him a lucrative deal with PSV Eindhoven in Holland.

Stars of the Nineties

Romario was but one of the many bright

lights who brought the game into the 1990s. As in most major sports, the stars of soccer had begun to transcend the statistics, awards, and championships to which they contributed. They were now businesses unto themselves, corporate entities with a long chain of attorneys, agents, marketers, publicity people, and assorted hangers-on wagging beneath them. The off-field distractions were mighty, which meant that the most successful players were not always the ones who possessed the greatest skill, but the ones who could march onto a field, switch into soccer mode, and just play the game.

Among these stars was a quartet of Latin Americans who gave Romario a run for his money, including fellow Brazilian, Careca. He had established his scoring talents during World Cup '86 with five goals and carried Brazil's lowly Guarini club to the national title in 1987-88. He then transferred to Naples, where he teamed with Maradona to deliver the 1989 UEFA Cup and 1990 Italian league championship. In 1993, Careca moved to the Hitachi club, where he was instrumental in broadening the soccer horizons of Japanese fans. The most recognizable of the four players was Colombia's Carlos Valderrama, whose wild hairdo and all-around game earned him high praise in the late 1980s, including South American Footballer of the Year. He won the award again in 1994, when he took the lightly regarded national team through the qualifiers—including an unforgettable 5-0 blanking of Argentina—all the way to an unexpected berth in the World Cup.

Uruguay turned out its best player in years in the person of Enzo Francescoli, whose skills sparked a bidding war between his country's two great clubs, Peñarol and Nacional. In the end, it was River Plate of

Ruud Gullit watches a downfield pass. The dreadlocked Dutch player was World Footballer of the Year in 1987 and 1989. In 1988, he captained Holland to the European Championship.

Argentina that won his services, and he rewarded them by becoming the top player in South America in 1984. He soon took his act to France, where he led Marseilles to a league championship in 1989–90. Mexico produced its finest player of the 1980s in striker Hugo Sanchez. In the late 1980s and early 1990s, he led the Spanish league in goals five times in a row, and after each he would execute an acrobatic somersault taught to him by his sister, an Olympic gymnast.

In Europe, Holland continued to come up with new stars, including Ruud Gullit, whose dreadlocks made him one of the most recognizable players in the game. He was also one of the most talented, winning World Footballer of the Year in 1987 and 1989 and European Footballer of the Year in 1987 after AC Milan paid a record fee of about $10 million to obtain his services from the Eindhoven club. In 1988, he led Milan to the European Cup and captained the Dutch team to victory in the European Championship. The man who scored an unforgettable goal during that final was Marco van Basten, who also teamed with Gullit in Milan. Van Basten was a tall, lanky player who fashioned his game after Johan Cruyff's, and he collected nearly as many awards as the legendary Dutchman. He was European Footballer of the Year in 1988, 1989, and 1992 and World Footballer of the Year in 1988 and 1992. Rounding out the Dutch team during this period was Dennis Bergkamp, an unconventional striker who preferred to let things develop in front of him before entering the fray. A world-class player for Amsterdam's Ajax club while still in his teens, Bergkamp transferred to Italy's Internazionale club for about $12 million in 1992.

France continued to field strong teams during the late 1980s and 1990s thanks to a pair of emerging stars. Eric Cantona, one of the modern era's legendary bad boys, bounced from club to club, alternating between disciplinary squabbles and fantastic on-field successes. After playing for five different teams by the age of 25, he joined Leeds United and helped them win the English First Division title in 1992. He then moved over to Manchester United, which won the division in 1993 and 1994. Jean-Pierre Papin became one of the top strikers in the game, leading the French league in goals four consecutive seasons and being named European Footballer of the Year before transferring to AC Milan in 1992, where he played in his second European Cup final in three seasons.

Elsewhere in Europe, Denmark boasted two fine players in Michael Laudrup and Peter Schmeichel, and Enzo Scifo bounced between clubs in Belgium, Italy, and France.

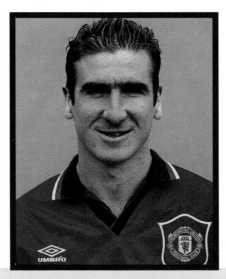

Eric Cantona was voted Sir Matt Busby Player of the Year in 1995–96. Despite his bad-boy antics, Cantona was one of the world's premier players in the 1980s and 1990s.

Laudrup helped Juventus to the World Club Cup in 1985 then transferred to AC Barcelona, where he helped the team win the European Cup in 1992. A squabble with the national manager kept him out of the 1992 European Championships, but his younger brother, Brian, proved an excellent replacement with his attacking play. Schmeichel could lay claim to being the top goalkeeper of the 1990s, especially after his clutch saves enabled the Danes to win the 1992 European Championship. Scifo, who was born in Belgium to Italian parents, claimed Belgian citizenship at the age of 18 so he could play in the 1984 European Championship, but his style was more suited for Italian soccer. That is just where he ended up, carving out a nice career as a midfielder for Internazionale before playing several years in France.

Italy kept bringing new players into the picture, with Franco Baresi and Roberto Baggio having the greatest impact at the international level. Baresi's skill as a sweeper enabled him to win a spot on the national team in 1987, where he proved the equal of Gullit and Van Basten in his ability to both defend and attack against the best teams in the world. He played his entire career with AC Milan and was the chief cause for their success in the 1980s. Baggio was Italy's most beloved superstar after Maradona fell from grace, and his sale to Juventus in 1990 sparked three days of rioting by disappointed fans in Florence, where he had risen to prominence. Voted World and European Footballer of the Year in 1993, Baggio led Juventus to the 1993 UEFA Cup and took the Italian team to the very brink of another World Cup in 1994.

Spain's Emilio Butragueño was the top young player in Europe during the mid-1980s, and he stepped up to superstar status during World Cup '86 when he riddled the Danish defense with four goals in a second-round match. Butragueño's teammate with Real Madrid, the midfielder Michel, also ranked among the top players in the game. In neighboring Portugal, Paulo Futre was busy making his reputation as an inspirational leader, taking FC Porto to a 1987 European Cup win. Futre went to Atletico Madrid a few weeks later and thrived there for six seasons, then went to three teams in the course of a year, eventually ending up with the Reggiana club in Italy. Sadly, he blew out his knee after scoring his first Italian league goal.

Great Britain was especially fertile ground for soccer talent during the late 1980s and early 1990s, producing no less than eight world-class players. The two

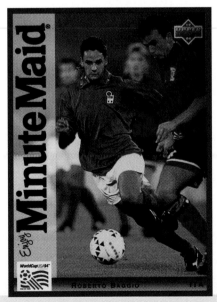

This trading card was distributed in conjunction with Minute Maid for World Cup '94. It shows the degree to which corporate sponsorship touches every level of soccer.

biggest names were Gary Lineker and Paul Gascoigne. Lineker, who rose from the humblest of beginnings, remained humble and gracious despite the fact he was feted as soccer's unstoppable scoring machine. Lineker netted 48 international goals—one short of the national record—and led the English First Division in scoring with three different clubs. Among his other highlights was an FA Cup triumph and a hat trick against Real Madrid while playing for AC Barcelona. Though just as popular, Gascoigne was the flip side of Lineker. A reckless midfielder whose emotional play often led to injury or suspension, Gascoigne was a magnet for disaster, whether in games, at practice, or during a night on the town. He became something of a cult figure during World Cup '90, when he burst into tears after being tossed from the game at a crucial moment in the semifinal against Germany. Gascoigne played in Italy from 1992 to 1995, then returned to England with the Rangers, leading them to the 1996 league championship.

The other top players from the British Isles included Northern Ireland's Norman Whiteside, who at 17 became the youngest player ever to appear in the World Cup, and Welshmen Neville Southall and Ian Rush. Southall earned English Footballer of the Year honors with Everton in 1985 and led the club to the FA Cup in 1984 and to the European Cup-Winners' Cup in 1985. Rush rivaled Lineker as a scorer in the 1980s and enjoyed tremendous success as the focal point of a Liverpool team that dominated the English league standings throughout the decade. Rounding out this group were Ally McCoist and Paul McStay from Scotland, and Paul McGrath, who battled through injuries to become one of Ireland's most beloved stars. McCoist rose to prominence with the Rangers, the top club in the Scottish league for a decade, thanks to his talent as a striker. McStay, a playmaking midfielder, spent his entire career with the Celtic club, playing in the shadow of McCoist and the Rangers but nevertheless distinguishing himself as one of the top men in the game.

West Germany remained a soccer superpower, thanks to the development of two brilliant players in the late 1980s. Midfielder Lothar Matthäus got his first taste of the big time as a substitute on his country's 1980 European Cup–winning team. By 1986, he was one of the game's brightest young stars, distinguishing himself time and again in World Cup play and later winning honors as European Footballer of the Year. Jürgen Klinsmann, a deadly striker, was the German league's top scorer in the late 1980s before moving to Italy with Inter Milan. There, he blossomed into an international superstar with his special knack for getting open. Unlike most players at his position, who make use of their speed by simply running up and down the field, Klinsmann worked in circles to disrupt the defense. These two made up the core of the West German World Cup team in 1990, along with veteran striker Rudi Völler and Pierre Littbarski, who once said his aim in life was to dribble past all 10 opponents, fake out the goalie, and put the ball in the net with a back heel.

World Cup '90

Unfortunately, there would be no such offensive fireworks at World Cup '90, which by all accounts was a dreadful tournament. Instead of focusing on attack, the top teams concentrated on eliminating mistakes. Needless to say, goals were few and far between, and in this atmosphere of tentative offense and tight, hard-tackling defense, the world's best players rarely shone. One notable exception was Cameroon's dynamic squad, led by Roger Milla. In the opening round, Africa's top team ran circles around defending champion Argentina and went on to beat Colombia in extra time to reach the quarter-finals. There Milla and company opened a 2-1 lead on England, which barely averted disaster in a 3-2 win in extra time.

The English team, led by Gascoigne and Lineker, earned its semifinal berth after David Platt shocked Belgium with a magnificent volley off Gascoigne's free kick in the final minute of extra time. Against Cameroon, Platt scored once and Lineker twice on penalty kicks, after being dragged down in the box on two occasions. Gascoigne moved the team through the tournament, playing the best soccer of his career. But in the semifinal against West Germany, Gascoigne was left sobbing after being booked for a silly foul, while his teammates lost a dramatic shootout and a chance to make the final for the first time since 1966.

The West Germans had reached the semifinal with their customary efficiency, their lone blemish being a 1-1 tie with Colombia. In that game, the irrepressible Valderrama was carried off the field, but later returned to score the equalizer. Against its old World Cup enemy, Holland, West Germany played perhaps the most exciting match of the tournament. The 2-1 nail-biter, won by the Germans, was especially interesting to the Italian fans because, during the regular season, three of the top Dutch players performed for AC Milan while three of the best Germans played for Italian league rival Internazionale.

Facing them in the final was Argentina.

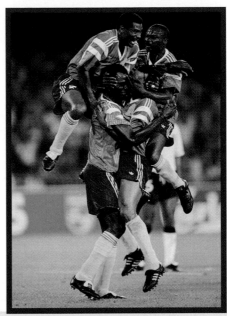

Cameroon's national team celebrates a goal during World Cup '90. Africa's best team defeated defending champion Argentina and a powerful Colombian team before losing in the quarterfinals.

The team's star, Maradona, was only playing at half speed due to injury, and its other top player, Claudio Cannigia, was not allowed to play because he had accumulated too many yellow cards.

Thanks largely to their brilliant goalic, Sergio Goycochea, the Argentines squeaked past Yugoslavia and Italy in ugly games that had to be decided on penalty kicks after extra time to set up a rematch of the 1986 final. Although many of the same players were in uniform, the game lacked the drama and class of that contest. Play was dull and conservative, with coaches Franz Beckenbauer and Carlos Bilardo instructing their players to concentrate on defense. With Maradona neutralized, Argentina had no offense. West Germany, however, refused to press the attack, choosing instead to wait for a break. It came in the form of a penalty kick with six minutes to go. The match ended 1-0, and everyone went home wondering what had become of the "simplest game."

Soccer Takes on the United States

If soccer was going to catch on in the United States, it most certainly would have to put on a better show than it had in Italy. Americans would not and could not be romanced by a sport that featured such uninspired play. Much educating would have to be done by World Cup '94, along with a lot of convincing. To most people in the United States, soccer was a game that kids played. Most people had no interest in the sport, could not name an active world-class player, and were completely unaware that the World Cup was even coming to the United States. When soccer news did find its way into the nightly sports report, it usually had to do with fan violence or stadium disasters. When sports fans flipped past soccer games on the television dial, the announcers were usually speaking Spanish. In other words, although the eyes of soccer would soon be upon the United States, it was still "foreign" to U.S. fans in almost every way.

The crazy thing was that most countries beg FIFA to allow it to host the World Cup. Yet now FIFA—desperately anxious to establish a foothold in the United States—essentially was begging the United States to host the event. FIFA even changed its rules to make the games more appealing to American fans. The offside rule was relaxed to make it more like hockey's, incentives were created to keep teams from settling for a tie, and violent tackles would be met with an immediate ejection. Also, injured players would be hustled off the field for treatment so the game could continue; American sports fans—used to continuous high-speed collisions in hockey and football—had no patience for some guy writhing around on the grass for two minutes because he had been kicked in the shins.

Meanwhile, the United States had to go about the business of assembling a team. This time it would be easier than in the past, for as host country the United States was guaranteed a spot among the 36 finalists. Every soccer player in the country had their eyes on World Cup '94, as well as those Americans playing abroad in professional leagues. In the spring of 1991, the United States Soccer Federation hired Bora Milutinovic as its coach. He had a reputation as a miracle worker, guiding Mexico to the quarterfinals at World Cup '86 and coaxing wins over Scotland and Sweden from an underdog Costa Rican squad at World Cup '90. No host country had ever failed to reach the second round, he was constantly reminded, and despite the long odds, he was not about to go down in history as the first coach to bow out in the opening round.

Drawing mainly on a mixed bag of players from colleges, local clubs, and regional pro leagues, Milutinovic began molding a club and building a system that would maximize America's advantages—size, strength, and athleticism—while masking its many weaknesses. The main weakness, of course, was that U.S. teams could never seem to win against international opponents. Since 1950, Team USA's most significant victory had come against Trinidad and Tobago in 1989. It was a mild upset, but it was good enough to earn the team a berth in World Cup '90. But there they were routed by the Czechs,

Italians, and Austrians in the first round. This problem beating quality teams could not be masked; it had to be remedied.

The process began in 1991, when the United States toppled Mexico 2-0 in the CONCACAF Gold Cup. So embarrassed was the Mexican coach that he quit the next day: that's how lightly regarded the Americans were just three years prior to World Cup '94. The team continued to improve, as Milutinovic shuffled players in and out, looking for winning combinations. In 1992, Team USA beat Ireland, which had reached the quarterfinals of World Cup '90, and tied Italy 1-1 to win the U.S. Cup, a relatively new competition that had begun to draw top teams and players from around the world. In an exhibition against European Cup champion AC Milan, the U.S. squad battled to another 1-1 tie. And at U.S. Cup 1993, Team USA dumped England 2-0, making headlines in Europe and even making a few sports pages in the United States.

During this time, several leading players emerged. Lightning-quick midfielder Cobi Jones brought crowds to their feet with his end-to-end runs, giving the national team an offensive boost in several key matches in the three years preceding World Cup '94. A walk-on at UCLA in the late 1980s, Jones could probably have played professionally overseas but chose instead to work with Team USA. Alexi Lalas, whose long beard and shock of red hair made him the most-recognized Team USA member, exhibited a knack for being in the right place at the right time. His first international goal came in the 2-0 shocker against England, and he rode the crest of that achievement to become a team leader. Voted the nation's top college player in 1991, Lalas proved fearless on defense and a classic opportunist on offense.

U.S. national team defender Alexi Lalas patrols the field.

Goalie Tony Meola, a tremendous natural athlete, established himself as the number-one goalie and team captain despite feuding with Milutinovic. His commitment to the World Cup dream led him to decide to drop out of the University of Virginia after winning NCAA Player of the Year honors in 1990, and his international experience made him the perfect man to work between the posts.

In the spring of 1994, Milutinovic began putting the final touches on his team. With the European season over, he finally had access to all of his top players. John Harkes, Tab Ramos, Roy Wegerle, Eric Wynalda, Paul Caliguri, and Thomas Dooley would round out the squad and lend the team a little international experience. Harkes was a key figure on Team USA, having played in England for several years. The midfielder's 30-yard shot to beat Peter Shilton was voted 1991 goal of the year in England, and he participated in the UEFA Cup with the Sheffield Wednesday club in 1992. Ramos, whose father played professionally in

The U.S. national team poses for a photograph before a World Cup '94 match.

Uruguay, had performed well at World Cup '90 and signed on with a Spanish team. Wegerle would be counted upon for his scoring. The NASL's last Rookie of the Year in 1984, he went on to star for the Queens Park Rangers. Wynalda also was a scorer, netting nine goals in his first 10 games with the Saarbruecken club of the German league in 1992. Like Meola, he had dropped out of college to play for Team USA in World Cup '90. Caliguri was the man who scored the goal against Trinidad and Tobago that got Team USA into World Cup '90. He also enjoyed success with several clubs in Germany during the late 1980s and early 1990s. Finally, in Dooley, America had a legitimate veteran of international competition. In the German league, he had been pulling down more than $250,000 a year, but he signed to play with Team USA for less than a third of that amount. He instantly became the team's best all-around performer, winning Player of the Year honors in 1993.

Besides training with Team USA, the players worked tirelessly in clinics around the country to generate interest and excitement for the sport. With the additional efforts of the new, market-savvy USSF president—Alan Rothenberg, who promised that a new professional league would arise in the wake of World Cup '94—soccer in the United States was finally getting its foot in the door. On the eve of the World Cup, half of Americans polled said they were now interested in the game. And about a third said they intended to watch the World Cup. Those numbers promised to increase if Team USA made it past the first round, putting a little extra pressure on Milutinovic and his players. Of course, none of these young men played on a par with the stars they would face at World Cup '94, but they understood how a team can be far greater than the sum of its parts, and they were all willing to do whatever it took to make that happen.

World Cup '94

World Cup '94 was viewed as a three-way affair, with Germany, Brazil, and Italy as favorites. Argentina and Holland were also given outside shots at making it to the final, as was the Colombian team, led by Carlos Valderrama, Freddy Rincon, and Faustino

During a World Cup '94 match, Bulgaria's Hristo Stoitchkov tries to curl a free kick over a wall of German defenders as goalkeeper Bodo Illgner tries to catch a glimpse of the ball.

Asprilla. They were the class of Group A, a seeming shoo-in to reach the second round. But things went badly for the Colombians. First, they dropped a 3-1 shocker to a Rumanian team led by midfielder Gheorghe Hagi. Next, against Team USA, the Colombians again played lackluster ball and lost 2-1 after center-back Andres Escobar mistakenly booted the ball into his own net. That loss put Colombia out of the tournament, and a few days later, Escobar was murdered when he returned to his country. The crime was committed on the streets of Medellín, Colombia's drug-trafficking capital. Speculation was that Escobar's murder came at the hands of enraged drug lords, who had lost millions betting on the national team.

Meanwhile, Team USA was the toast of the tournament. Prior to the victory against Colombia, they had tied the Swiss team 1-1. That gave the United States enough points to make it to the second round, where they faced Brazil. In a tightly played match, Team USA held its own before bowing 1-0 to the tournament favorite.

Brazil rode the fine play of its dynamic duo, Romario and Bebeto, reaching the final by defeating Holland in the quarterfinals and Sweden in the semis. There, they did not face Argentina or Germany, as anticipated, but an Italian team that had narrowly averted disaster three times. In the opening round, Italy lost to Ireland, edged Norway 1-0, and gained a tie with Mexico to squeak into round two. There they were two minutes away from defeat at the hands of Nigeria when Roberto Baggio tied the game and then scored the winner in extra time. Baggio continued to shine in the quarterfinals with the deciding goal in a 2-1 win over Spain. In the semifinals, Italy faced the surprising Bulgarian squad, which had previously disposed of Germany. Billed as a match between the immense talents of Hristo Stoitchkov and

Baggio, the Italians prevailed 2-1 on two goals from their red-hot striker to reach the final. As for Argentina, they too proved to be underachievers, falling to Romania in round two after their star, Maradona, failed a drug test and was removed from the team.

Despite the black eyes of the Escobar and Maradona incidents, FIFA officials were very pleased with the matchup for the final. In Brazil, American audiences would see the smart, stylish attack of Romario, Bebeto, and Rai, backed by Claudio Taffarel, the country's best goalie in 20 years. Italy, on the other hand, played tough, aggressive, European-style soccer. The team also had the air of an over-achieving underdog, which U.S. sports fans have always loved. As game time approached, however, Italy had to deal with a couple of

France scores a goal against Spain during the 1996 European Cup tournament.

problems. Baggio had hurt his hamstring against Bulgaria and would not be at full speed. Also, the veteran sweeper Franco Baresi was reinserted into the lineup after having undergone arthroscopic surgery to repair a knee injury suffered in the first round.

The result was a classic duel between a high-powered offense and a stingy defense, with Brazil attacking and Italy biding its time until they detected a mistake. After 90 minutes, the match was scoreless, although Brazil had some great chances, including a ball that squirted through the hands of Gianluca Pagliuca and banged against the post. In two extra periods, both teams came close to scoring, with Baggio and Romario both missing by inches. Thus for the first time, the World Cup final was decided by a penalty-kick shootout. Baresi missed the goal with his shot, but Pagliuca evened things up by stopping a blast from Marcio Santos. After each team scored twice, Brazil prevailed when Taffarel saved a shot by Daniele Massaro and Baggio sent his shot just over the bar.

A Bright Future

As soccer nears the end of the 20th century, it is bigger, stronger and more popular than ever. New communications technologies have made more information and more games available to fans on a worldwide basis and have put millions of fans in touch with one another. That can only spell further success in the next century, for perhaps more than any other sport, the fans have always been an integral part of the game. They send a charge through the stadium that the players can and do feel down on the field, and they fill the air with their cheers, their songs, their cries of joy, and their screams of agony.

What lies ahead for the game? The spread of soccer should soon encompass almost every developed country in the world, including the United States. With the establishment of a new professional circuit, Major League Soccer (MLS), and more than 13 million young people playing the sport, all the elements are there for soccer some day to establish a presence comparable to that of football, baseball, basketball, and hockey. Along the Pacific Rim, where soccer has been picking up

Arash Nuamouz of the L.A. Galaxy takes down Jaime Moreno of D.C. United in the 1996 MLS championship game. D.C. United won the league's first championship 3-2.

The action is spirited during a youth soccer game in Palisades Park, New Jersey. Throughout the 1980s and 1990s, soccer has increased in popularity as a participation sport for young players.

momentum for a quarter-century, an explosion in popularity seems just around the corner.

Who are the emerging superstars who will take the game into the 21st century? With more people in more countries playing the game, there are more world-class players populating more professional clubs and national teams than ever before. Among the most promising are Brazil's Ronaldo, Spain's Raul, France's Zinedine Zidane, and Argentina's stars Hernan Crespo and Ariel Ortega. And, of course, there is always the

next Pelé, the next Beckenbauer, the next Maradona waiting to burst upon the scene and assume his place among soccer's all-time greats. As the mantel of stardom is passed from one generation to the next, as the game grows in popularity and intensity in even the most remote reaches of the world, one is always reminded that, both literally and figuratively, the sun will never set on soccer. Right now—at this very moment, in fact—someone, somewhere is playing the game. And that cannot be said about any other sport.

Modern Soccer Timeline

1848 The first rules for soccer are drawn up at Cambridge University, in England.

1855 The Sheffield Football Club—the oldest team still in existence—is formed.

1863 The Football Association is formed on October 26.

1866 Offside rule dictates that three defensive players must be between an offensive player and the goal.

1867 The Queen's Park Football Club—the oldest Scottish team still in existence—is formed.

1871 The FA Cup is established.

1872 Scotland and England meet in soccer's first international match.

1873 The Scottish Football Association is formed.

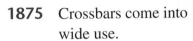

1874 Players begin wearing shin guards, which are strapped on over the socks.

1875 Crossbars come into wide use.

1876 The Football Association of Wales is formed.

1878 Referees begin using whistles. The first night game is played between two Sheffield clubs.

1879 The Pietermaritzburg County club, Africa's first, is formed in Natal, South Africa.

1880 The Irish Football Association is formed. The first Australian football club is formed in Sydney.

1883 The first British International Championship is held. The two-handed throw-in replaces the one-handed method.

1885 Professional soccer is legalized in England.

1886 Caps for international appearances are awarded for the first time.

1887 Soccer is introduced to Russia.

1888 The Football League is formed.

1890 The Irish League and Scottish League begin play.

1891 Umpires are replaced by more specialized referees and linesmen. The penalty kick is instituted. The Peñarol football club is formed in the Uruguayan capitol of Montevideo.

1892 The Football League's Second Division is formed. Goal nets, first introduced in 1890, are used in the FA Cup final for the first time.

1893 The Scottish League accepts professionals for the first time.

1896 The length of international matches is fixed at 90 minutes.

1897 The Corinthians club tours South America. The Juventus club is formed in Turin, Italy.

1898 The Players' Union is formed to protect the rights of soccer players.

1899 Promotion and relegation system begins in English soccer.

1900 The Bayern Munich football club is formed in Germany, and Ajax Amsterdam begins play in Holland.

1901 The first 100,000-plus crowd attends the FA Cup final. The River Plate club in founded in Argentina.

1902 The Real Madrid club is formed in Spain. Austria plays Hungary in the first non-British international match. Women's soccer clubs are excluded from the Football Association. A women's team from Preston, England, tours the United States.

1904 FIFA is formed in Paris on May 21. The Benfica football club is founded in Lisbon, Portugal.

1905 South America sees its first international match, between neighbors Argentina and Uruguay.

1908 England plays its first international match in Europe, beating Austria in Vienna. The United Kingdom defeats Denmark to win the first Olympic gold medal in soccer.

1909 The Eastern League is formed among semipro teams in New York, New Jersey, and Pennsylvania.

1910 Argentina defeats Uruguay for the first South American Championship.

1911 Stanford University institutes the first collegiate soccer program west of the Mississippi.

1912 A rule limiting the goalkeeper's use of hands to within the penalty area is introduced. England beats Denmark again to win the Olympic gold medal. The Santos football club is founded in Brazil.

1913 The United States Soccer Federation is founded. China plays the Philippines in Asia's first international match.

1916 The first South American Championships are held.

1920 Belgium defeats Czechoslovakia to win the Olympic gold medal. A women's match between England and France draws more than 10,000 spectators. The Australian Football Association is formed.

1921 The American Soccer League begins play.

1923 Egypt becomes the first African country to join FIFA.

1924 Uruguay defeats Switzerland to win the Olympic gold medal.

DIXIE DEAN

1925 New offside law leads to a goal-scoring explosion.

1926 A match between German-American all-stars and a visiting Austrian club draws 35,000, a U.S. record that stands for nearly 50 years.

1927 The Mitropa Cup begins. The Cardiff club of Scotland becomes the first non-English team to win the FA Cup. Play-by-play of a soccer match—Sheffield United vs. Arsenal—is broadcast on radio for the first time.

1928 Dixie Dean scores 60 goals in a season, a Football League record. Uruguay defeats Argentina for its second consecutive Olympic gold medal.

1929 England suffers its first defeat on European soil, dropping a match to Spain, 4-3.

1930 Host country Uruguay wins the first World Cup.

1932 Substitutions are allowed for the first time in international matches.

1933 Uniform numbers are worn for the first time during an FA Cup final.

1934 Host country Italy wins the World Cup.

1936 Joe Payne scores 10 goals in a game, a Football League record. Italy beats Austria to win the Olympic gold medal.

1937 The official weight of a soccer ball is increased by an ounce.

1938 Italy wins its second consecutive World Cup. Scottish star Jimmy McGrory retires with 550 career goals, a Football League record. The FA Cup final is televised live for the first time.

1939 The Football League orders all players to wear uniform numbers.

1945 The Soviet Union's Moscow Dynamo club reignites soccer passion with a brilliant showing against top English clubs.

1947 Argentina wins the South American Championship for the third consecutive year.

1948 Sweden beats Yugoslavia to win the Olympic gold medal.

1949 Argentine soccer players go on strike, with many joining teams in other countries. The Italian champion Torino club is wiped out in an airplane crash.

1950 Uruguay wins the World Cup before a record crowd of 203,500. England enters the tournament for the first time and loses to the lightly regarded United States team.

1951 The white soccer ball first comes into use.

1952 England loses its first match against a European opponent on its own home soil, dropping a 6-3 decision to Hungary in Wembley Stadium. Yugoslavia is runner-up once more, as Hungary wins the Olympic gold medal.

1953 Argentine superstar Alberto Di Stefano transfers to Real Madrid, becoming the cornerstone of the decade's most dominant club.

1954 West Germany wins the World Cup. England falls to Hungary in Budapest 7-1, its most lopsided international defeat. UEFA is formed.

1956 Real Madrid club wins the first European Cup. English star Stanley Matthews wins the first European Footballer of the Year award. The Soviet Union defeats Yugoslavia for the Olympic gold medal.

1957 John Charles becomes the first English superstar to transfer to a foreign club. Egypt wins the first African Nations Cup.

1958 Eight Manchester United players, including budding superstar Duncan Edwards, die in an airplane crash in Munich, West Germany. Brazil, inspired by teenage sensation Pelé, wins the World Cup. French striker Just Fontaine scores a World Cup record 13 goals. The first European Championships are played.

1959 St. Louis University wins the first NCAA soccer championship.

1960 The USSR wins the first European Nations Cup. Peñarol club of Uruguay wins the first Copa Libertadores. Real Madrid wins its fifth consecutive European Cup and the inaugural World Club Cup championship. Yugoslavia reaches the Olympic gold medal game for the fourth consecutive time and finally wins the gold, downing Denmark 3-1.

1961 The Fiorentina club of Italy wins the first European Cup Winners' Cup.

1962 Brazil repeats as World Cup champion, defeating Czechoslovakia.

1964 Three hundred and eighteen people die in history's worst soccer disaster as a disallowed goal sparks rioting during a game between Peru and Argentina. Hungary defeats Czechoslovakia to win the Olympic gold medal.

1965 Stanley Matthews becomes the first soccer player to be knighted.

1966 England defeats West Germany to win the World Cup, the first final ever televised in the United States. Portuguese star Eusebio scores nine goals during the competition.

1967 The number of substitutions allowed in international play is increased from one to two.

1968 Italy wins the first European Football Championship. Portuguese star Eusebio wins the first Golden Boot award as the leading goal scorer in Europe. Hungary repeats as Olympic gold medalist, defeating Bulgaria. Red and yellow cards are introduced during competition. The North American Soccer League begins play. England's Football Association recognizes women's soccer.

1970 Brazil beats Italy to win the World Cup for the third time, retiring the Jules Rimet Trophy. West Germany's Gerd Müller scores nine goals during the competition.

1971 Women's Football Association is founded in England, and an unofficial women's world championship is held for the first time in Mexico City.

1972 Poland defeats Hungary 2-1 in the Olympic gold medal final.

1973 Holland's Ajax club wins its third consecutive European Cup. Kyle Rote, Jr., wins the NASL scoring

title and is named Rookie of the Year.

1974 West Germany, led by sweeper Franz Beckenbauer, wins the World Cup. The United States Soccer Football Association changes its name to the United States Soccer Federation.

1975 Brazilian superstar Pelé joins the NASL's New York Cosmos. The NASL championship is renamed the Soccer Bowl.

1976 The Bayern club of Munich wins the European Cup for the third consecutive time. Chile's Elias Figueroa wins his third consecutive South American Footballer of the Year award. East Germany wins Olympic gold, defeating Poland in the final.

1977 Franz Beckenbauer joins the New York Cosmos, leads the team to the NASL championship, and wins Player of the Year honors.

1978 Argentina wins the World Cup. The Football League lifts its longtime ban on foreign players. The Major Indoor Soccer League begins play.

1979 Soccer is banned in Iran after fundamentalist leader Ayatollah Kohmeini seizes power from the Shah of Iran.

1980 Czechoslovakia defeats East Germany to win the Olympic gold medal. The World Club Cup is renamed the Tokyo Cup and moved permanently to Tokyo, Japan.

1981 The NCAA sanctions the first women's soccer championship.

1982 Aston Villa becomes the sixth consecutive English winner of the European Cup.

1984 France wins the European Championship, its first international title. France tops Brazil for the gold medal at the Los Angeles Olympics.

1985 Michel Platini of Italy's Juventus club is named European Footballer of the Year for the third consecutive season. Nigeria becomes the first African country to win an international championship in FIFA's first Under-17 World Cup.

1986 Argentina, inspired by Diego Maradona, wins the World Cup.

1988 Eight years after a special ruling by FIFA, the Olympics feature world-class pros for the first time.

The Soviet Union beats Brazil for the gold medal. The United Sates is named host country for World Cup '94.

1989 The United States upsets Trinidad and Tobago to qualify for its first World Cup finals since 1950.

1990 Franz Beckenbauer becomes the first to win a World Cup as a player and as a manager, as he pilots West Germany to victory over Argentina in the final.

1991 Michelle Akers leads the United States to the first Women's World Cup. Superstar Diego Maradona is suspended for 15 months after failing a drug test. FIFA suspends Iraq after dictator Saddam Hussein orders invasion of neighboring Kuwait.

1992 England creates the new Premier League, reducing the Football League to 71 clubs across three divisions. Spain edges Poland in front of a wild home crowd to win the Olympic gold medal.

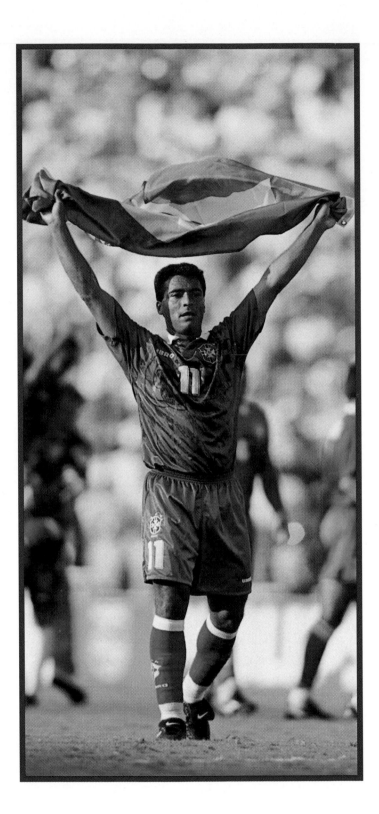

1993 Women's soccer is officially added as a medal sport for the 1996 Olympics.

1994 Brazil defeats Italy as the World Cup is decided by a penalty shootout for the first time.

1995 Liberian superstar George Weah is named World Footballer of the Year.

1996 Major League Soccer begins play as North America's newest professional soccer league, D.C. United, led by Jeff Agoos, wins the first MLS Cup. Approximately 75,000 fans watch the U.S. Women's team defeat China 2-1 to win the Olympic Gold Medal. Nigeria wins the gold medal in the men's competition.

1997 Members of the Iraqi National team are caned after failing to qualify for World Cup '98.

1998 The World Cup is held in France.

APPENDIX A
The World Cup

Year	Champion	Runner-Up	Score	Host Country
1930	Uruguay	Argentina	4-2	Uruguay
1934	Italy	Czechoslo-vakia	2-1*	Italy
1938	Italy	Hungary	4-2	France
1950	Uruguay	Brazil	2-1	Brazil
1954	West Germany	Hungary	3-2	Switzer-land
1958	Brazil	Sweden	5-2	Sweden
1962	Brazil	Czechoslo-vakia	3-1	Chile
1966	England	West Germany	4-2*	England
1970	Brazil	Italy	4-1	Mexico
1974	West Germany	Netherlands	2-1	West Germany
1978	Argentina	Netherlands	3-1*	Argentina
1982	Italy	W. Germany	3-1	Spain
1986	Argentina	W. Germany	3-2	Mexico
1990	West Germany	Argentina	1-0	Italy
1994	Brazil	Italy	3-2‡	United States

* Decided in extra time
‡ Decided by penalty kicks after extra time

APPENDIX B
European Cup

Year	Club	Country
1956	Real Madrid	Spain
1957	Real Madrid	Spain
1958	Real Madrid	Spain
1959	Real Madrid	Spain
1960	Real Madrid	Spain
1961	Benifica	Portugal
1962	Benifica	Portugal
1963	AC Milan	Italy
1964	Inter Milan	Italy
1965	Inter Milan	Italy
1966	Real Madrid	Spain
1967	Celtic	Scotland
1968	Manchester United	England
1969	AC Milan	Italy
1970	Feyenoord	Holland
1971	Ajax Amsterdam	Holland
1972	Ajax Amsterdam	Holland
1973	Ajax Amsterdam	Holland
1974	Bayern Munich	West Germany
1975	Bayern Munich	West Germany
1976	Bayern Munich	West Germany
1977	Liverpool	England
1978	Liverpool	England
1979	Nottingham Forest	England
1980	Nottingham Forest	England
1981	Liverpool	England
1982	Aston Villa	England
1983	SV Hamburg	Germany
1984	Liverpool	England
1985	Juventus	Italy
1986	Steaua Bucharest	Romania
1987	Porto	Portugal
1988	PSV Eindhoven	Holland
1989	AC Milan	Italy
1990	AC Milan	Italy
1991	Red Star Belgrade	Yugoslavia
1992	Barcelona	Spain
1993	Olympique Marseille	France
1994	AC Milan	Italy
1995	Ajax Amsterdam	Holland
1996	Juventus	Italy
1997	Borussia Dortmund	Germany

APPENDIX C
Copa Libertadores
(South American Club Cup)

Year	Club	Country
1960	Peñarol	Uruguay
1961	Peñarol	Uruguay
1962	Santos	Brazil
1963	Santos	Brazil
1964	Independente	Argentina
1965	Independente	Argentina
1966	Peñarol	Uruguay
1967	Racing Club	Argentina
1968	Estudiantes	Argentina
1969	Estudiantes	Argentina
1970	Estudiantes	Argentina
1971	Nacional	Uruguay
1972	Independiente	Argentina
1973	Independiente	Argentina
1974	Independiente	Argentina
1975	Independiente	Argentina
1976	Cruzeiro	Brazil
1977	Boca Juniors	Argentina
1978	Boca Juniors	Argentina
1979	Olimpia	Paraguay
1980	Nacional	Uruguay
1981	Flamengo	Brazil
1982	Peñarol	Uruguay
1983	Gremio	Brazil
1984	Independiente	Argentina
1985	Argentina Juniors	Argentina
1986	River Plate	Argentina
1987	Peñarol	Uruguay
1988	Nacional	Uruguay
1989	Atletico Nacional	Colombia
1990	Olimpia	Paraguay
1991	Colo Colo	Chile
1992	Sao Paulo	Brazil
1993	Sao Paulo	Brazil
1994	Velez Sarsfield	Argentina
1995	Gremio	Brazil
1996	River Plate	Argentina
1997	Cruzeira	Brazil

APPENDIX D
World Club Cup

Year	Club	Country
1960	Real Madrid	Spain
1961	Peñarol	Uruguay
1962	Santos	Brazil
1963	Santos	Brazil
1964	Inter Milan	Italy
1965	Inter Milan	Italy
1966	Peñarol	Uruguay
1967	Racing Club	Argentina
1968	Estudiantes	Argentina
1969	AC Milan	Italy
1970	Feyenoord	Holland
1971	Nacional	Uruguay
1972	Ajax Amsterdam	Holland
1973	Independente	Argentina
1974	Atletico de Madrid	Spain
1975	(Tournament not held)	
1976	Bayern Munich	West Germany
1977	Boca Juniors	Argentina
1978	(Tournament not held)	
1979	Olimpia	Paraguay
1980	Nacional	Argentina
1981	Flamengo	Brazil
1982	Peñarol	Uruguay
1983	Gremio	Brazil
1984	Independente	Argentina
1985	Juventus	Italy
1986	River Plate	Argentina
1987	Porto	Portugal
1988	Nacional	Uruguay
1989	AC Milan	Italy
1990	AC Milan	Italy
1991	Red Star Belgrade	Yugoslavia
1992	Sao Paulo	Brazil
1993	Sao Paulo	Brazil
1994	Velez Sarsfield	Argentina
1995	Ajax Amsterdam	Holland
1996	Juventus	Italy
1997	Borussia Dortmund	Germany

APPENDIX E
European Cup-Winners' Cup

Year	Club	Country
1961	AC Fiorentina	Italy
1962	Atletico Madrid	Spain
1963	Tottenham Hotspur	England
1964	Sporting Lisbon	Portugal
1965	West Ham	England
1966	Borussia Dortmund	West Germany
1967	Bayern Munich	West Germany
1968	AC Milan	Italy
1969	Slovan Bratislava	Czechoslovakia
1970	Manchester City	England
1971	Chelsea	England
1972	Glasgow Rangers	Scotland
1973	AC Milan	Italy
1974	Magdeburg	East Germany
1975	Dynamo Kiev	USSR
1976	Anderlecht	Belgium
1977	SV Hamburg	West Germany
1978	Anderlecht	Belgium
1979	Barcelona	Spain
1980	Valencia	Spain
1981	Dynamo Tblisi	USSR
1982	Barcelona	Spain
1983	Aberdeen	Scotland
1984	Juventus	Italy
1985	Everton	England
1986	Dynamo Kiev	USSR
1987	Ajax Amsterdam	Holland
1988	Mechelen	Belgium
1989	Barcelona	Spain
1990	Sampdoria	Italy
1991	Manchester United	England
1992	Werder Bremen	Germany
1993	Parma	Italy
1994	Arsenal	England
1995	Real Zaragoza	Spain
1996	Paris St. Germain	France
1997	FC Schalke	Germany

APPENDIX F
European Championship

Year	Champion	Runner-Up	Score
1960	USSR	Yugoslavia	2-1
1964	Spain	USSR	2-1
1968	Italy	Yugoslavia	2-0
1972	West Germany	USSR	3-0
1976	Czechoslovakia	West Germany	2-2*
1980	West Germany	Belgium	2-1
1984	France	Spain	2-0
1988	Holland	USSR	2-0
1992	Denmark	Germany	2-0
1996	Germany	Czech Republic	2-1

* won on penalty kicks after extra time

APPENDIX G
European Footballer of the Year

Year	Player	Club
1956	Stanley Matthews	Blackpool
1957	Alfredo Di Stefano	Real Madrid
1958	Raymond Kopa	Real Madrid
1959	Alfredo Di Stefano	Real Madrid
1960	Luis Suarez	Barcelona
1961	Omar Sivori	Juventus
1962	Josef Masopoust	Kukla Prague
1963	Lev Yashin	Moscow Dynamo
1964	Dennis Law	Manchester United
1965	Eusebio	Benifica
1966	Bobby Charlton	Manchester United
1967	Florian Albert	Ferencvaros
1968	George Best	Manchester United
1969	Gianni Rivera	AC Milan
1970	Gerd Müller	Bayern Munich
1971	Johan Cruyff	Ajax
1972	Franz Beckenbauer	Bayern Munich
1973	Johan Cruyff	Barcelona
1974	Johan Cruyff	Barcelona
1975	Oleg Blokhin	Dynamo Kiev
1976	Franz Beckenbauer	Bayern Munich
1977	Allan Simonsen	Borussia Moenchengladbach
1978	Kevin Keegan	SV Hamburg
1979	Kevin Keegan	SV Hamburg
1980	Karl-Heinz Rummenigge	Bayern Munich
1981	Karl-Heinz Rummenigge	Bayern Munich
1982	Paolo Rossi	Juventus
1983	Michel Platini	Juventus
1984	Michel Platini	Juventus
1985	Michel Platini	Juventus
1986	Igor Belanov	Dynamo Kiev
1987	Ruud Gullit	AC Milan
1988	Marco Van Basten	AC Milan
1989	Marco Van Basten	AC Milan
1990	Lothar Matthaus	Inter Milan
1991	Jean-Pierre Papin	Olympique Marseille
1992	Marco Van Basten	AC Milan
1993	Roberto Baggio	Juventus
1994	Hristo Stoitchkov	Barcelona
1995	George Weah	AC Milan
1996	Matthias Sammer	Borussia Dortmund
1997	Ronaldo	FC Barcelona

APPENDIX H
South American Footballer of the Year

Year	Player	Club
1971	Tostao	Cruzeiro
1972	Teofilo Cubillas	Alianza Lima
1973	Pelé	Santos
1974	Elias Figueroa	Internacional
1975	Elias Figueroa	Internacional
1976	Elias Figueroa	Internacional
1977	Zico	Flamengo
1978	Mario Kempes	Valencia
1979	Diego Maradona	Argentinos Juniors
1980	Diego Maradona	Boca Juniors
1981	Zico	Flamengo
1982	Zico	Flamengo
1983	Socrates	Corinthians
1984	Enzo Francescoli	River Plate
1985	Julio Cesar Romero	Fluminese
1986	Antonio Alzamendi	River Plate
1987	Carlos Valderrama	Deportivo Cali
1988	Ruben Paz	Racing Buenos Aires
1989	Bebeto	Vasco Da Gama
1990	Raul Amarilla	Olimpia
1991	Oscar Ruggeri	Velez Sarsfield
1992	Rai	Sao Paulo
1993	Carlos Valderrama	Junior Barranquilla
1994	Cafu	Sao Paulo
1995	Enzo Francescoli	River PLate
1996	Ronaldo	FC Barcelona

APPENDIX I

World Footballer of the Year

Year	Player	Country
1982	Paolo Rossi	Italy
1983	Zico	Brazil
1984	Michel Platini	France
1985	Michel Platini	France
1986	Diego Maradona	Argentina
1987	Ruud Gullit	Holland
1988	Marco Van Basten	Holland
1989	Ruud Gullit	Holland
1990	Lothar Matthaus	West Germany
1991	Jean-Pierre Papin	France
1992	Marco Van Basten	Holland
1993	Roberto Baggio	Italy
1994	Paolo Maldini	Italy
1995	Gianluca Viali	Italy
1996	Ronaldo	Brazil

APPENDIX J

FIFA World Footballer of the Year

Year	Player	Country
1991	Lothar Matthaus	Germany
1992	Marco Van Basten	Holland
1993	Roberto Baggio	Italy
1994	Romario	Brazil
1995	George Weah	Liberia
1996	Ronaldo	Brazil

For More Information

Books

Abangama, Julius. *Soccer for Beginners: How to Understand & Play the Game* (Silver Spring, MD: Allied, 1994).

Arnold, Caroline. *Pelé: The King of Soccer* (Danbury, CT: Watts, 1991).

Brown, Michael. *Soccer Techniques in Pictures* (New York: Perigee, 1991).

Gutman, Bill. *Soccer* (Tarrytown, NY: Marshall Cavendish, 1990).

Howard, Dale E. *Soccer Around the World* (Danbury, CT: Children's Press, 1994).

———. *Soccer Stars* (Children's Press: Danbury, CT: 1994).

Pollock, Bruce. *Soccer for Juniors* (New York: Simon and Schuster, 1980).

Ventura, Anthony. *Soccer, Play Like a Pro* (Mahway, NJ: Troll, 1990).

Wilner, Barry. *Soccer* (Milwaukee: Gareth Stevens, 1995).

———. *Soccer* (Austin, TX: Raintree/Steck-Vaughn, 1993).

For Advanced Readers

Gardner, Paul. *The Simplest Game: An Intelligent Fan's Guide to the World of Soccer* (New York: Macmillan, 1994).

Harris, Larry R. *Futbol Means Soccer: Easy Steps to Understanding the Game* (Manhattan Beach, CA: Soccer for America, 1978).

Rollin, Jack. *World Cup 1930–1990* (New York: Facts On File, 1990).

Synder, John S. *Goal! Great Moments in World Cup History* (San Francisco: Chronicle Books, 1994).

Internet

Because of the changeable nature of the Internet, sites appear and disappear very quickly. These resources offered useful information on soccer at the time of publication. Internet addresses must be entered with capital and lowercase letters exactly as they appear.

http://www.yahoo.com
The Yahoo directory of the World Wide Web is an excellent place to find Internet sites on any topic.

http://www.fifa.com/index.html
The official FIFA home page provides up-to-the-minute information about the World Cup and World Cup qualifying matches and links to other excellent soccer sites.

http://www.france98.com/english/index.html
This is the official web site dedicated to World Cup 1998 in France.

http://www.mlsnet.com/
The official home page of Major League Soccer provides the latest news and results from the MLS. Check out the Kidzone!

http://www.soccer.org/
This is the official web site of the American Youth Soccer Association, which sponsors soccer programs for more than 560,000 players ages 4 to 18 in more than 900 regions across the United States.

http://www.cris.com/~Jg189/wsf/
This site, sponsored by the Women's Soccer Foundation, provides lots of information about women's soccer.

http://www.canoe.ca/SoccerCanada/home.html
This is the official web site of the Canadian Soccer Association.

Index

Page numbers in *italics* indicate illustrations.

About the Author

Mark Stewart ranks among the busiest sportswriters of the 1990s. He has produced hundreds of profiles on athletes past and present and authored more than 40 books, including biographies of Jeff Gordon, Monica Seles, Steve Young, Hakeem Olajuwan, and Cecil Fielder. A graduate of Duke University, he is currently president of Team Stewart, Inc., a sports information and resource company located in Monmouth County, New Jersey.